AF530481

Rare Gems

a non-vegetarian gourmet collection from Maharashtra

Reprinted in 2024

Om Books International

Corporate & Editorial Office
A-12, Sector 64, Noida 201 301
Uttar Pradesh, India
Phone: +91 120 477 4100
Email: editorial@ombooks.com
Website: www.ombooksinternational.com

Sales Office
107, Ansari Road, Darya Ganj, New Delhi 110 002, India
Phone: +91 11 4000 9000
Email: sales@ombooks.com
Website: www.ombooks.com

Food photography: Michael Swamy
Travel photography: Michael Swamy, Ganesh Shedge & Chaitanya Naik
Food styling: Michael Swamy & Mugdha Savkar
Research: Aditya Mehendale, Sagar Naik & Mrunal Savkar
Editor: Rita D'Souza
Book design: Ajay Mago & Shraboni Roy

ISBN 978-93-84625-21-4

Printed in India

10 9 8 7 6 5 4 3

Rare Gems

a non-vegetarian gourmet collection from Maharashtra

Aditya Mehendale

Foreword
Prakash Javadekar

Om Books International

Contents

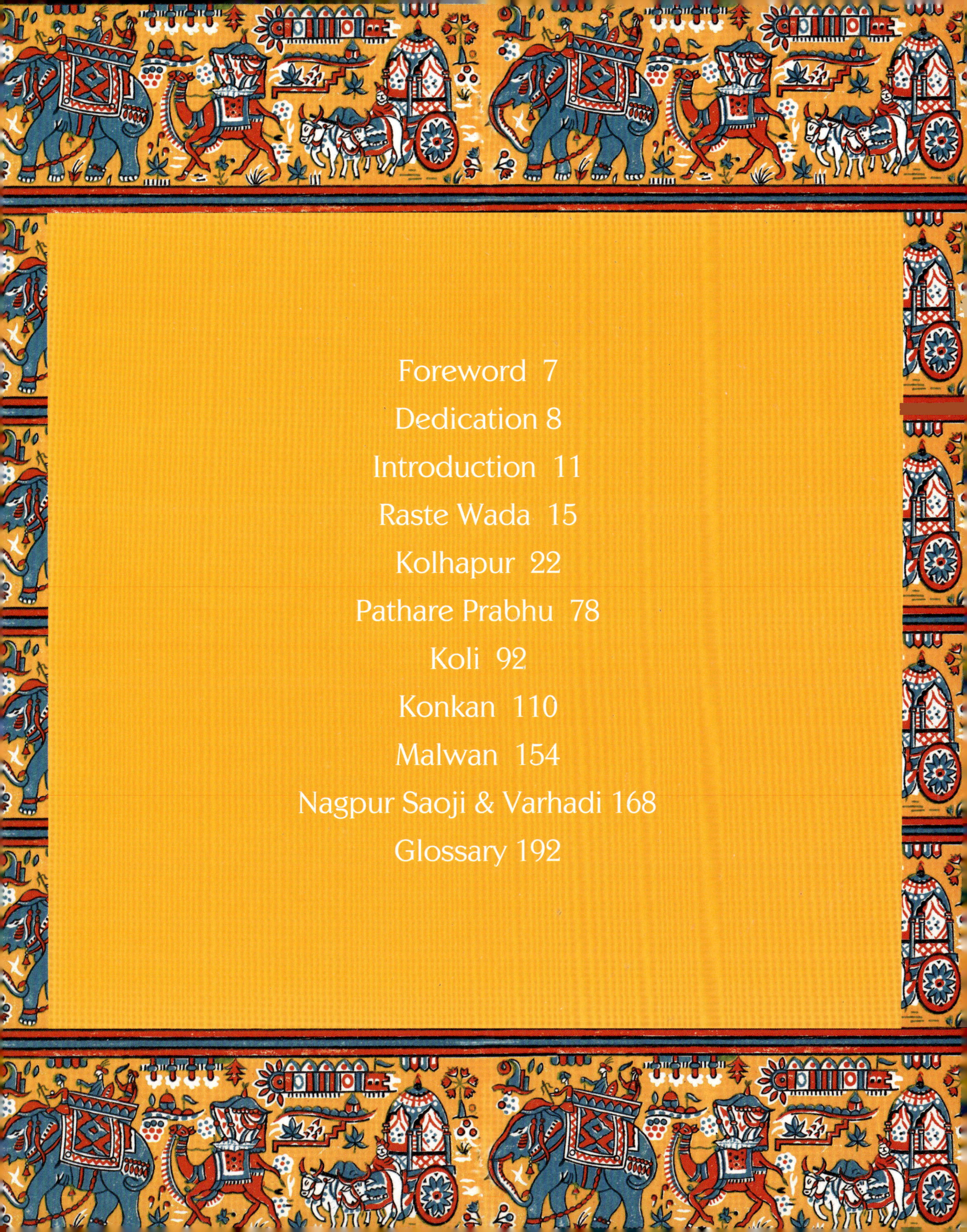

Foreword

Maharashtra – a land recognised for its rich culture, heritage, spirituality and simplicity. However, a less celebrated fact is that it is equally rich in its tradition of food.

That, precisely, was the reason for my interest in writing the foreword for my dear friend Aditya Mehendale's book. The concept of this book appeals to me largely as it showcases the lesser-known dishes, not only from the homes of Maharashtrian nobility, but also from the rural and coastal communities of the state.

I also feel proud to be a part of this effort initiated by Aditya, as this exclusive book will now help in uncovering the rich Maharashtrian culinary traditions, of particularly non-vegetarian food, not only across other Indian states but also the globe over.

I have relished most of these dishes at one time or another during our long association, and know that they will bring you great enjoyment and a real taste of Maharashtra.

Prakash Javadekar
Minister of State for Environment,
Forest and Climate Change (Independent Charge),
Government of India

Late Shri Shankar Rao Wakalkar

Late Smt. Maisaheb Bavdekar

Late Sardar Anandrao Raste

For my beloved wife Tarita, who adds strength to my skills, colour to my being, flavour to my meals, and love to every moment of togetherness

Introduction

If you do what you love, everyone will love what you do!

That is what I have always believed and that is what drew me to the kitchen. It is hard to remember when I first fell in love with the art of cooking. It was probably around the same time that I started my ardent love affair with eating good food!

As a child, I was fortunate enough to experience some of the greatest cuisines, elaborately presented by passionate cooks on my maternal grandfather's wada (estate) in Pune, where I spent my childhood. My visits to the kitchen gave me a chance to closely observe the intricate cooking techniques and blending of flavours. With the culinary intellect by which I was surrounded, I was fortunate to witness both the veneration of tradition, and the art of innovation. I consider myself blessed, for rarely does one get such an opportunity to cultivate one's passion.

As I grew up, the passion for food kept increasing. So did the demands of the palate! It was during my teen years, that my manservant then, Laxman Kamble (Kamble Mama, as I fondly called him) would fulfill my impromptu, and sometimes even unrealistic, wishes for scrumptious non-vegetarian food. Kamble Mama also gave me the opportunity to explore the earthy flavours of food from the common man's kitchen. It was then I learnt that it is not using the richest ingredients to prepare a dish, but the love that goes into cooking it and serving it to your loved ones, that brings about the best taste.

The real turning point was when I got to share my passion for cooking with my grand-aunt Maisaheb Bavdekar. Though she was my grandfather's older sister, she was more like a friend and mentor to me. Her deep knowledge about different foods and spices constantly astounded me. She would talk proportions and the specific blending of spices when the chefs around her could barely name the dishes she had cooked over the years.

Most of my cooking is inspired by Mai Ajji's (Maisaheb Bavdekar) collection of recipes and my own zest for travelling. Whether it is hot Warhadi fare, soulful Saraswat

sauces, fiery Kolhapuri curries, mouth-watering Pathare Prabhu delicacies, simple Koli delights or tangy Malwani dishes, most of my recipes are a happy blend of both!

To me the kitchen is a place of recreation where I can forget my worries and relax to the symphony of clanking utensils, rumbling grinding stones and sizzling spices. It is therapeutic to experience the aromas of the various sauces simmering and the scent of searing spices filling the air.

This book is a humble attempt by an untrained cook like me to pass on my knowledge and passion to readers who share a similar love for authentic Maharashtrian non-vegetarian food. I hope to be your companion in your kitchen through the pages ahead, and also be a small part of the gratification that you witness in the hearts of your loved ones when you serve up these dishes.

You may serve any one or a mix of dishes from the different cuisines in the chapters to come, but one thing I would suggest is not to forget to garnish every dish with a smile. If you have enjoyed cooking it, they will enjoy every morsel. This is the only lesson that has helped me reach this stage of culinary merit, and I know it will enliven your journey from the supermarket to the kitchen table as well!

In conclusion, I would like to say that this book would not have come into being without the unstinting and generous support of Mr. Baba Jadhavrao and Dr. Ravikumar Jadhav, to whom I am deeply grateful.

Sardar Raste Family with staff (1940)

Raste Wada

I am a proud son of Maharashtra and an even prouder scion of the illustrious Raste family who were closely associated with the mighty Peshwas, the former rulers of the Maratha empire founded by Chhatrapati Shivaji Maharaj.

Bhikaji Shamrao Gokhale, originally from Velneshwar, in the Ratnagiri district of Maharashtra, was conferred the title of Raste ('rast' meaning 'pure' or 'fair' in Persian) by the Sultan of Bijapur, who found the moneylender and financier to be an honest and upright man. He gained favour with Chhatrapati Shahu Maharaj, the grandson of Chhatrapati Shivaji Maharaj, financing many of his campaigns and ventures, and moved with him to Satara when he established his court there. So close had they become, that Chhatrapati Shahu asked for Bhikaji's daughter Gopikabai's hand in marriage for his son Balaji Bajirao Peshwa, later called Nanasaheb Peshwa. The marriage was solemnised in 1730 in Bhikaji's impressive mansion in Wai, where Chhatrapati Shahu and family often stayed as guests. It was because of the marriage of their sister to the Peshwa scion that the Rastes became known as the mamas (maternal uncles) of the Peshwas.

The influence of Gopikabai's brothers in the Peshwa courts grew as her own status and power within the Peshwa family increased. She insisted that her two brothers, Madhavrao and Anandrao Raste, accompany her husband Nanasaheb Peshwa on his military campaigns in Karnataka, Gujarat and Malwa, and ensured they moved to Pune to remain always close to her and the centre of power.

Anandrao Raste, who became the commander-in-chief of the Peshwa cavalry, eventually, built Raste Wada an imposing mansion in an area called Shivpuri, which later became known as Raste Peth. The Rastes had a tradition of not only building grand homes for themselves, but also temples, watersheds and community structures for the benefit of the town, their employees and tenants. Their property in Wai with its sprawling mansions and gardens was the cynosure of all eyes and cost a tidy fortune in those days. In addition, the Raste family built many temples that dot Wai, the most impressive being the Kashivishveshvar temple, another temple dedicated to Mahalakshmi and one dedicated to Vishnu, all built by Anandrao Bhikaji Raste at a cost of, in those days, two to three lakh rupees each. The Rastes are believed to have spent a staggering sum of over 40 lakh rupees on all their building works in Wai.

Gopikabai's son, Madhavrao Peshwa, gifted lands all over the empire to his maternal uncles including the land on which the imposing Raste Wada in Pune was built. Anandrao Raste is believed to have spent nine lakh rupees on the mansion which must have been the envy of all. It took nine years to build and when it was completed, it was an impressive dwelling place spread over 11,000 square metres with an imposing five-storied main house, two large courtyards, many fountains and four water tanks. The main house, which comprised several large halls and many private rooms, had carved wooden pillars and beautifully sculpted stone carvings and limestone details around the latticed windows. Floral, animal and bird motifs were incorporated into the woodwork and limestone embellishments, while Belgian crystal chandeliers suspended from the elaborately carved ceilings gave the mansion an air of grandeur.

The estate housed several private temples, including a Shiva temple, as well as a mosque for the Muslim members of the

cavalry. The edges of the estate were lined with stables and coach houses for the hundreds of horses and carriages, with special deep stone water troughs nearby.

One of the most impressive features of Raste Wada was a six-kilometre long aqueduct built by Anandrao Raste which piped in a constant supply of fresh spring water all the way from the Kondhwa and Wanowrie hills. Some of that water flowed into a ten-foot deep copper-lined cistern in which water was heated for bathing and cooking. The kitchens were cavernous with many storerooms and separate areas for cooking, washing and grinding of spices.

Raste Wada was the laboratory for all my culinary explorations and experiments. The variety of cuisines turned out in the sprawling kitchens by a number of speciality cooks, and the cavernous storerooms with huge porcelain jars filled with the year's supply of grain and other necessities, as well as exotic ingredients sourced from all over the country and beyond, were a magical playground for my maturing taste buds. I liked nothing better than to spend my time messing about in the kitchens watching the cooks deftly plying their craft.

And there seemed to be hordes of them: at one time I can remember there were at least 30 cooks, each an expert in a particular cuisine or type of meal. One of the cooks was from Gwalior, who cooked dishes like lamb barbat, dal chicken, and kheema stuffed karela. One cook was Konkani, and another from Sangli who made pure Brahmin food. Each one was assigned a workplace, stove and assistants and turned out dish after delicious dish at a moment's notice. Ingredients were requisitioned by the cook from the storeroom and he then proceeded to grind the spices required for each dish. Food was cooked in mainly earthenware pots or seasoned copper utensils lined with tin, on coal or wood fires which gave the food an unparalleled smoky flavour.

The kitchens ran like well-oiled machinery to feed the over 100 residents of the wada including staff, and some who, like my grandfather, had very exacting standards and discerning palates.

Such smooth functioning involved good planning. Monthly menus were drawn up with different menus for different occasions. The menus for one of my grandfather's legendary bridge parties were very different from that of a birthday feast, Diwali dinner or a haldi-kumkum ceremony. Depending on the menu, a different cook was assigned charge of the kitchen for the event. For traditional banquets or pangats, silver utensils and platters were the order of the day. Meals were laid out on individual low tables before guests who sat cross-legged on decorative mats. The menu for these occasions would be extensive with as many as 26 dishes on offer.

Daily meals were relatively simple, with lunch consisting of a mutton dish, a seafood dish, two vegetables, lentils (dal), varan-bhaat, the staple lentil-rice combination, and bhakri or rice flatbreads. Vegetarian meals were a rarity, which is why I cannot imagine a meal without some form of meat, poultry or seafood. I also owe my penchant for non-vegetarian food to both my grandfather, Anandrao Raste and his sister, Maisaheb Bavdekar, who broke with tradition and started the practice of throwing lavish parties and feasts with a variety of meat and fish dishes on the menu.

Both Maisaheb and Anandrao shaped my culinary world. I developed my adventurous eating habits and curiosity for all things food from their own desire to expand their culinary horizons. An educationist who founded the Maisaheb Bavdekar Academy in Kolhapur, Maisaheb's enquiring mind led her not only to gain and spread academic knowledge, but to experience other cultures and food as well. Married to Pant Amatya Bhaiyasaheb Bavdekar, a descendant of Ramachandra Pant Amatya, the youngest minister in Shivaji's court, she travelled all over India and collected recipes from all the places she visited. No food was too humble for her interest and her discerning palate could help her to replicate unerringly whatever she tasted. She wrote copious notes about all her experiments with food and the dishes she had eaten. I was her favourite dining partner as we shared a common passion. I was overwhelmed when she presented me with her handwritten collection of recipes, many of which I have included in this book. They are a priceless legacy that I will always treasure.

I spent many happy hours at Raste Wada and at my grand-aunt's home in Kolhapur discovering the magical art and alchemy of cooking, which sowed the seeds for a life-long passion for food, and the development of a repertoire of eclectic dishes from all over Maharashtra, the rest of India, and indeed all over the globe.

My grandparents Sardar Anandrao Raste and Induraje Raste

Sardar and Induraje Raste at their wedding

With my sisters and pet dog 'Chhoti'

My great-grandmother Smt. Girijabai Raste with family and staff members

A formal lunch at Raste Wada

Women dining at Raste Wada

Top: With my father Shrikant Mehendale and mother Alka Mehendale

Right: The old letter box at Raste Wada, whispering the history of its glorious past

Kolhapur

KANDA-LASUN MASALA
BARODA PULAO
CHOPS TAWA FRY
KOLHAPURI KOMBDICHE SUKKE
KOLHAPURI KHEKDA RASSA
KAALA RASSA
PIVLA RASSA
KHULAA RASSA
BANGA RASSA
KAALE SUKKE
KOMBDICHE LAPCHAP
MARAL RASSA
KOLHAPURI DAHI MUTTON
HIRWA RASSA
MUTTONACHE TAAZE LONCHE
KOLHAPURI MUTTON LONCHE
NARALI KOMBDI
PANDHRA RASSA
TAMBDA RASSA
BHARLELI KOMBDI
KHIMYACHI PARSUNDI
GOLI PULAO
KOLHAPURI BADAK MASALA
KOLHAPURI MUTTON SUKKA
KOLHAPURI METHI MUTTON
KOLHAPURI LAHORI MASALA
KOLHAPURI KOMBDI DUM PULAO
GAOTHI KOMBDI RASSA
MUNDI RASSA

One wonders if the demon Kolhasura, for whom Kolhapur was named as a dying wish granted by the goddess Mahalaxmi, had anything to do with the fiery food served there. The tongue-searing dishes, cooked traditionally with the lethal tiny lavangi mirchi, have given Kolhapuri food the reputation of being one of the most challenging cuisines of India. That Kolhapur also produces some of the purest jaggery, and the freshest, creamiest milk and yoghurt, is somehow lost in the clamour over the pungency of the curries.

Having grown up around spicy food, I sometimes wonder what all the fuss is about, but admit that a somewhat tempered version will allow many more to enjoy the complex interplay of spices that make up a good Kolhapuri curry, like the iconic tambda and pandhra rassas. Kolhapur is, in many ways, second home to me as my grand-aunt, Maisaheb Bavdekar, lived there. She was my culinary hero and inspiration and much of what I know about food is what I learned from her at Kolhapur, which is why I have begun this collection with Kolhapuri recipes.

Kolhapur, in southwestern Maharashtra, has played an important role in the history of the state. It was once an important centre of the Maratha Empire, became the scene of battle against the Mughals, and later was absorbed into the British Empire, all of which had an influence on the food which developed into a rich cuisine with a royal lineage and an underlying hearty common touch.

At my grand-aunt's home there was an air of sanctity around formal and celebration meals. Guests were seated cross-legged on paats (low seats). Sacred verses were chanted at the start of the meal, which was served in silver thalis (plates) and bowls placed on chowrangs (low tables). A variety of vegetables, meats and lentils were served one after the other, with rice, bhakris (rice flatbread) or wheat chapattis, and an array of chutneys and pickles, of which Kolhapuri thecha (green chilli chutney) is a favourite.

Meat, especially goat meat or mutton, offal and game formed an important part of our meals. Shikar (hunting) was a regular pastime, and it was common to serve wild boar, quail, partridge, venison and other game in the days before hunting was banned. In our home, non-vegetarian dishes outnumbered the vegetarian ones, especially as vegetables were cooked with a little meat or seafood to add flavour!

The truth is that Kolhapuri food gets most of its flavour from the panoply of spices that go into its basic spice blend. Kanda- lasun masala (onion-garlic spice mix) is an amalgam of a long list of spices, roasted onion, garlic and coconut. It is what gives Kolhapuri dishes their characteristic heat and boldness. Today, the deadly lavangi mirchi is replaced with the milder Byadagi or Kashmiri chilli with a few fiery Sankeshwari chillies thrown in for good measure.

Yoghurt, made from fresh cow or buffalo milk, tempers the heat of some Kolhapuri dishes. Every evening, Kolhapuris wait for the cowherds to drive their cows or buffaloes through the main streets so that milk can be freshly drawn. Dudhkatta is the name for this unique tradition, which is particularly availed of by wrestlers who practise the art of kushti (wrestling), for which Kolhapur is famous, and who drink a couple of litres of the freshly drawn milk at one go every day.

Kolhapur's other culinary contribution is its fine quality jaggery. Black smoke rising out of sugar cane fields signals that a gurhal (jaggery processing plant) is doing its work turning sweet sugar cane juice into liquid gold jaggery. Some of it is sold as kakvi, a viscous liquid not unlike honey, and the rest pressed into blocks. All over Kolhapur you will find stalls selling fresh sugar cane juice spiked with ginger and lime, which is the perfect foil to all those rich red curries.

If you visit Kolhapur, do not miss out on the missal which is a multi-textured snack of spicy sprouted bean curry, topped with chopped onions, green chillies, ginger and garlic, smothered with a heap of crunchy spiced farsan or sev (gram flour crispies) with a sprinkling of fresh coconut for light relief. Although it is vegetarian, it is one of my favourite dishes, to which I try, sometimes unsuccessfully, not to add any fried meat or fish.

KANDA-LASUN MASALA

ONION AND GARLIC SPICE PASTE

This is a basic Kolhapuri spice blend that is made in large quantities to last the whole year. Preparing it is a time-consuming process, but a labour of love worth the effort. The process begins by drying the ingredients in the hot sun for a few days. Then comes the tedious task of removing the stalks of the chillies and peeling mounds of onions and garlic. Sometimes, the seeds of the chillies are removed so they do not tone down the deep red colour of the spice mix. The secret to increasing the shelf-life of the spice mix is to avoid any water at all and to fry the onions well. Apart from using this spicy blend in meat and vegetable dishes, I find it makes a delicious snack spread on jowar bhakris and drizzled with ghee.

Ingredients

DRY-ROASTED SPICE MIX
100g dried red Byadagi chillies
200g dried red Kashmiri chillies
2½ tablespoons cumin seeds
1 tablespoon coriander seeds
1 tablespoon sesame seeds
1 teaspoon black cumin seeds
1 tablespoon Indian bay leaves
Rock salt

FRIED SPICE MIX
Oil, as required
1 cup grated dried coconut
1 tablespoon black peppercorns
1 tablespoon cloves
1 tablespoon black cardamom pods
1 tablespoon star anise
1 teaspoon cassia buds
1 teaspoon asafoetida
1 tablespoon dried lichen

ONION MIX
Oil for deep-frying
250g onions, sliced
¼ cup garlic cloves, peeled
1 tablespoon grated ginger

Method

- For the dry-roasted spice mix, dry-roast the chillies in batches in a large wok. Set aside to cool. Dry-roast the rest of the spices, except the salt, till fragrant. Grind the roasted chillies and spices with the rock salt to a fine powder.
- For the fried spice mix, heat a little oil in a wok; fry each ingredient separately till fragrant, adding enough oil to fry each one. Cool and grind to a fine powder.
- For the onion mix, heat the oil in a wok; deep-fry the sliced onions in batches till golden brown. Drain on absorbent paper. Empty all but 2 teaspoons oil from the wok and fry the garlic and ginger for a minute. Grind the onions, garlic and ginger to a fine paste.
- Combine all the ground spice mixes, making sure they are well mixed. Mix in more salt if necessary. Store in an airtight container.

Makes about 500g

BARODA PULAO

SMOKED MUTTON PULAO WITH COCONUT AND FRAGRANT SPICES

A culinary example of unity in diversity, this pulao was the result of a combined effort of the Muslim and Hindu cooks of the Peshwa army, and is believed to have originated in the royal kitchens of Baroda. Prepared using a combination of cooking styles and flavours predominant in both communities, this dish uses dried coconut, not often found in pulaos or biryani.

Ingredients

RICE
15 dried red Kashmiri chillies
7 star anise
8 green cardamom pods
5 (2.5-cm) cinnamon sticks
3 onions, sliced
4 bay leaves
8 cloves
8 black peppercorns
1½ teaspoons fennel seeds
1½ teaspoons coriander seeds
500g long-grained rice
Salt

MUTTON
8 tablespoons ghee
3 tablespoons grated dried coconut
2 tablespoons poppy seeds, soaked
1 teaspoon cumin seeds
3 onions, sliced
1½ teaspoons turmeric powder
4 teaspoons red chilli powder
2 tablespoons ginger-garlic paste
1kg mutton on the bone, cut into 5-cm pieces
Salt
2 cups fried sliced onions
A large pinch of saffron, soaked in a little warm water
½ cup fried cashew nuts, plus to garnish
½ cup chopped coriander leaves, plus to garnish
½ cup grated fresh coconut, plus to garnish
A piece of charcoal

Serves 8

Method

- For the rice, tie all the ingredients, except the rice and salt, in a piece of muslin or cheesecloth to make a spice bundle; boil in 4 cups water for 10-12 minutes. Remove the potli and reserve the spices.
- Add the rice and salt to the spice-flavoured water and cook till almost done. Drain.
- For the mutton, heat 2 tablespoons ghee in a pan; sauté the reserved potli spices. Grind to a paste.
- Grind the dried coconut, soaked poppy seeds and cumin seeds with a little water to a fine paste.
- Heat 3 tablespoons ghee in a heavy-bottomed pan; add the onions and sauté till golden brown. Add the turmeric and chilli powders, and sauté for half a minute.
- Add the potli masala paste, the ginger-garlic paste and coconut paste; sauté till the ghee separates. Add the mutton with 1½ cups water and salt, and cook till the mutton is tender and the gravy coats the mutton.
- To assemble the pulao, sprinkle the fried onions over the cooked mutton and spread half the rice on top. Sprinkle the saffron water, cashew nuts, coriander leaves and grated coconut over the rice. Spread the remaining rice on top and drizzle with 2 tablespoons melted ghee.
- Fix some wholewheat dough to the rim of the pan; heat the charcoal over an open flame till red hot. Place it in a heatproof bowl and place the bowl on the rice. Drizzle the remaining ghee on the coal. When the charcoal starts smoking, cover the pan with a tight-fitting lid and seal it with the wholewheat dough.
- Place the pan on a griddle and cook for 20 minutes. Unseal the pan, and serve the pulao hot, garnished with cashew nuts, coriander and grated coconut.

CHOPS TAWA FRY

TWICE-COOKED MUTTON CHOPS

This recipe brings back many fond memories of a feast I enjoyed at the table of Kapsekar Sardar, a descendant of a commander in the Peshwa army. Of all the delicacies laid out, this one was my favourite. The technique used to make this dish is unlike that used in other Maharashtrian meat dishes: the marinated chops are cooked in a heavy pan and then fried on a griddle over high heat till crisp on the outside.

Ingredients

2 tablespoons black peppercorns
1 tablespoon cloves
2 tablespoons green cardamom pods
2 tablespoons black cardamom pods
6 (2.5-cm) cinnamon sticks
1 whole nutmeg
1 tablespoon mace
2kg double mutton chops
Salt
Juice of 2 limes
2 tablespoons ginger-garlic paste
1 cup fresh coriander paste
1 cup fresh mint paste
3 cups yoghurt, whisked
½ cup green chilli paste
1 tablespoon Red Chilli Paste*
Oil for shallow-frying
Onion rings and lime wedges, to serve

Method

- Dry roast the peppercorns, cloves, green and black cardamoms, cinnamon, nutmeg and mace in a frying pan or griddle till fragrant. Cool and grind to a fine powder.
- Marinate the meat in a mixture of the spice powder and the rest of the ingredients, except the oil, for 2 hours.
- In a thick-bottomed pan, cook the marinated chops with a little water till tender and the water has evaporated.
- Heat the oil on a griddle, and fry the chops in batches till brown on both sides.
- Serve hot with onion rings and lime wedges.

Serves 8

*RED CHILLI PASTE

Boil 6 dried red chillies in 1 cup water for 6-8 minutes till soft. Drain, cool and grind to a paste. Remove seeds for a milder paste.

Makes ¼ cup

KOLHAPURI KOMBDICHE SUKKE

STIR-FRIED SPICY CHICKEN

The term 'sukka' denotes a dry dish without any gravy. Konkan and Maharashtrian cuisines are famous for their sukkas, prepared from vegetables, meat or fish. This chicken dish from Kolhapur is redolent of fenugreek and curry leaves, tempered with tamarind, giving it a spicy, tangy flavour that is lip-smackingly good.

Ingredients

SPICE PASTE

2½ tablespoons grated dried coconut
8 garlic cloves
½ tablespoon fenugreek seeds
1 teaspoon turmeric powder
1 teaspoon cumin powder

CHICKEN

2½ tablespoons oil
8 dried red Kashmiri chillies
1 tablespoon coriander seeds
1½ teaspoons cumin seeds
¾ teaspoon fenugreek seeds
¾ teaspoon mustard seeds
5 onions, finely chopped
2 tablespoons ginger-garlic paste
1kg chicken, cut into 10-12 pieces
2 tablespoons tamarind pulp
Salt
1 teaspoon turmeric powder
4 tablespoons ghee
10 curry leaves
Coriander leaves, to garnish

Method

- For the spice paste, grind the ingredients coarsely without adding any water.
- For the chicken, heat the oil in a pan; add the red chillies, coriander seeds, cumin seeds, fenugreek seeds and mustard seeds, and sauté for a few seconds. Add 1 chopped onion and ginger-garlic paste and sauté till the onion is golden brown.
- Add the chicken and sauté on high heat till the water has dried and chicken is tender, adding a little water if necessary so the chicken does not burn. Stir in the spice paste, tamarind pulp, salt and turmeric; cook till the gravy has dried and coats the chicken.
- Heat the ghee in a frying pan; add the remaining 4 chopped onions and sauté till brown. Add the curry leaves and sauté for 2 minutes. Add the onions and curry leaves to the chicken and stir to mix.
- Serve hot, garnished with chopped coriander leaves.

Serves 8

KOLHAPURI KHEKDA RASSA

CRAB CURRY

This robust curry owes its full-bodied flavour to the addition of 'crab juice,' in place of the usual stock or water. The smaller claws of the crab are blended to a paste that is strained through cheesecloth and added to the curry, giving it an unparalleled depth of crab flavour.

Ingredients

SPICE PASTE

1 cup grated dried coconut, roasted
10 black peppercorns
2 tablespoons poppy seeds, roasted

CRAB CURRY

1kg crabs
4 tablespoons oil
4-5 onions, chopped
1 tablespoon ginger-garlic paste
1 tablespoon Kanda-Lasun Masala (page 25)
1½ tablespoons Garam Masala (page 34)
1½ tablespoons red chilli powder
1½ teaspoons Goda Masala*
1½ teaspoons coriander powder
Salt
¾ cup kokum pulp
Chopped coriander and grated coconut, to garnish

Method

- Grind the ingredients for the spice paste.
- Clean and cut the crabs in half and remove the small claws. Grind the claws with 1 cup water. Strain through a piece of cheesecloth or muslin and reserve the water.
- Heat the oil in a large pan; add the onions and sauté till brown. Add the ginger-garlic paste, kanda-lasun masala and the ground spice paste; sauté for half a minute. Add the garam masala, chilli powder, goda masala and coriander powder, and stir to mix.
- Add the crab, salt, kokum pulp and reserved claw extract. Cook till the crab is tender.
- Serve hot, garnished with chopped coriander leaves and grated coconut.

Serves 6

*GODA MASALA

Heat 2-3 tbsp oil and fry 10 Kashmiri chillies, 1 cup coriander seeds, 1 tbsp cumin seeds, 6 (2.5-cm) cinnamon sticks, 12 cloves, 6 black cardamom pods, 1½ tsp black cumin seeds, 1½ tsp dried lichen, 1½ tsp cassia buds, 1 tsp asafoetida, 3-4 Indian bay leaves, 1 tsp mace. Dry-roast 1 cup grated dried coconut and ½ cup sesame seeds. Grind all spices together to a fine powder. Store in an airtight container. Makes about 500g

KAALA RASSA

BLACK MUTTON CURRY

This is a Kolhapuri delicacy that is not for the faint-hearted, as goat's blood is a major ingredient, giving the dish a blackish tinge. Animal blood is prized for its unique flavour and texture; think British black pudding, Tamil Nadu's aattu ratha poriyal and traditional Goan sarapatel. This Kolhapuri favourite also owes its intense hue and smoky flavour to the charring of ingredients including coconut, goat's spleen, onions and poppy seeds.

Ingredients

1kg mutton on the bone, cut into 5-cm pieces
1½ tablespoons ginger-garlic paste
1½ teaspoons turmeric powder
Salt
2 onions
½ dried coconut
50g goat's spleen
1 tablespoon sesame seeds
1 tablespoon poppy seeds
1 cup goat's blood
Juice of 1 lime
½ cup oil
1½ tablespoons Kanda-Lasun Masala (page 25)
1½ teaspoons Garam Masala*
Chopped coriander, to garnish

Method

- Marinate the mutton in a mixture of ginger-garlic paste, turmeric and salt.
- Roast the onions, coconut and goat's spleen separately on a griddle till charred. In a frying pan, roast the sesame seeds and poppy seeds till dark brown. Grind all the roasted ingredients to a fine paste.
- Steam the goat's blood together with the lime juice for 15 minutes; grind to a paste.
- Heat the oil in a pan; add the coconut paste, kanda lasun masala, garam masala and salt and sauté till the oil separates. Add the mutton and blood paste and sauté for 2 minutes. Add salt and 2 cups water and cook till the mutton is tender. Add more water if necessary, as the curry should be thin.
- Serve hot, garnished with chopped coriander leaves.

Serves 8

*GARAM MASALA

Dry-roast 4 tbsp coriander seeds, 1 tbsp cumin seeds, 1 tbsp black peppercorns, ½ tbsp black cumin seeds, ½ tsp cloves, 5-cm cinnamon stick, 4 large bay leaves, 4 black cardamom pods. Cool and grind to a fine powder. Makes about 1/3 cup

PIVLA RASSA

Yellow Mutton Curry

As its name suggests, this is a bright yellow curry owing mainly to the use of turmeric. My grandfather, whose refined sense of taste was legendary, would allow no other turmeric in his kitchens other than that from the town of Wai in Maharashtra, which was known to produce the best quality turmeric. And to maintain the sunny yellow colour of the curry, any ingredient which would alter the colour even slightly, such as red chillies or browned onions, was eschewed.

Ingredients

1kg mutton on the bone, cut into 5-cm pieces
1 tablespoon ginger-garlic paste
1½ tablespoons split pigeon peas
1½ tablespoons split Bengal gram
1½ tablespoons split green gram
4-5 tablespoons oil
5 onions, grated
10 black peppercorns
3 (2.5-cm) cinnamon sticks
6 cloves
6 green cardamom pods
2 bay leaves
1 tablespoon turmeric powder
1 tablespoon cumin powder
2 tablespoons coriander powder
1½ teaspoons Garam Masala (page 34)
Salt
10 green chillies, slit
Chopped coriander, to garnish

Method

- Rub the mutton all over with the ginger-garlic paste and leave to marinate for 30 minutes.
- Cook the split lentils in water till soft; purée or mash till smooth.
- Heat the oil in a pan; add the grated onion and sauté till pink. Do not let them brown. Add the peppercorns, cinnamon, cloves, cardamoms and bay leaves and sauté till fragrant. Add the turmeric powder, cumin powder, coriander powder, garam masala and salt, and stir to mix.
- Add the mutton and sauté for 5 minutes. Add 2 or 3 cups water and the mashed lentils, and cook till the mutton is tender. The curry should be thin. Add the slit green chillies and cook for 5 minutes.
- Garnish with chopped coriander and serve with boiled rice, rice bhakri or wholewheat rotis.

Serves 8

KHULAA RASSA

MUTTON IN TOMATO GRAVY

The name of this dish translates as 'mad curry' because it contains tomatoes, which were considered to be both introduced by the British, for whom the locals had little respect, and a serious departure from traditional methods of cooking. Kolhapuri cooks declared that only an unbalanced mind would suggest using tomatoes, which would lead to food spoilage, in place of tamarind or other local souring agents with time-tested preservative qualities, hence the name.

Ingredients

½ fresh coconut, grated
½ dried coconut, grated
6 onions, 3 sliced and 3 finely chopped
5 tablespoons oil
2½ tablespoons Hirwa Watan*
1½ tablespoons Kanda-Lasun Masala (page 25)
½ tablespoon Garam Masala (page 34)
1½ teaspoons turmeric powder
1½ tablespoons red chilli powder
1 cup fresh tomato purée
1kg mutton on the bone, cut into 5-cm pieces
Salt
Chopped coriander leaves, to garnish

Method

- Dry-roast the fresh and dried coconut and the sliced onions on a griddle till brown. Grind to a fine paste.
- Heat the oil in a pan; sauté the chopped onions till brown. Add the ground paste, hirwa watan, kanda-lasun masala, garam masala, turmeric and chilli powders, and the tomato purée; sauté till the oil separates.
- Add the mutton and salt and sauté for a few minutes. Add 2 cups water and cook till the mutton is tender.
- Garnish with chopped coriander and serve with rice or sorghum bhakri.

Serves 8

*HIRWA WATAN (Green Spice Paste)
Grind 1 cup green coriander, 4 green chillies, 20 garlic cloves, 5-cm piece ginger to a fine paste. Store in the refrigerator for up to 5 days. Makes about ½ cup

BANGA RASSA

GOAT OFFAL CURRY

I associate this dish with a great deal of digestive discomfort, as this impossibly delicious dish was cooked only occasionally. So whenever it was prepared, I would feast on it like there was no tomorrow, resulting in a situation of happy heart, heavy stomach! The original banga rassa is made with tripe, lungs and intestines with a few pieces of mutton added. In this recipe I have used mutton with liver, heart and kidneys, which many people find more palatable.

Ingredients

SPICE POWDER

1 tablespoon black peppercorns
1 tablespoon cloves
1 tablespoon black cumin seeds
1½ teaspoons cumin seeds
1 tablespoon coriander seeds
4 (2.5-cm) cinnamon sticks

SPICE PASTE

3 tablespoons oil
2 onions, sliced
1½ teaspoons sesame seeds
1 tablespoon poppy seeds
1 cup grated dried coconut

CURRY

500g goat offal (liver, heart and kidneys), chopped
1½ tablespoons vinegar
4 tablespoons oil
4 onions, finely chopped
1½ teaspoons ginger-garlic paste
2½ tablespoons red chilli powder
1kg mutton, cut into pieces
Salt
Chopped coriander leaves, to garnish

Method

- Dry-roast all the ingredients for the spice powder on a griddle. Cool and grind to a fine powder.
- For the spice paste, heat the oil in a frying pan and sauté the onions, sesame seeds, poppy seeds and grated coconut till brown. Grind to a fine paste.
- For the curry, in a pan cook the offal with vinegar and water for 10 minutes. Remove from the heat and drain.
- Heat the oil in a separate pan; add the chopped onions and sauté till brown. Add the ginger-garlic paste, chilli powder and ground spice powder, and sauté for half a minute.
- Add the cooked offal, chopped mutton and salt, and sauté for a few minutes. Add 2 cups water and cook till the meat is half done. Add the spice paste and cook till the meat is tender.
- Garnish with coriander leaves and serve with wholewheat roti or rice.

Serves 8

KAALE SUKKE

MUTTON WITH ROASTED CINNAMON, CHARRED ONION AND COCONUT

Cinnamon is the star of this dish. It not only lends its warm aroma but a sweet spiciness that beautifully complements the smoky flavour of charred coconut, onion and garlic.

Ingredients

7 onions
3 whole garlic bulbs
½ dried coconut
8 (2.5-cm) cinnamon sticks
1kg mutton on the bone, cut into 5-cm pieces
2 cups yoghurt, whisked
Salt
1½ tablespoons oil

Method

- Over an open flame, individually roast 4 whole unpeeled onions, the garlic bulbs and coconut till charred (see below). Remove the burnt skin from the onion and garlic.
- Dry-roast the cinnamon sticks in a frying pan till fragrant.
- Grind the roasted onions, garlic, coconut and cinnamon to a fine paste.
- Combine the yoghurt, salt and ground paste in a bowl. Mix in the mutton and leave to marinate for 30 minutes.
- Slice the remaining onions. Heat the oil in a pan; add the sliced onions and sauté till brown. Add the marinated mutton and very little water. Cook till the mutton is tender and gravy dry.
- Garnish with coriander leaves and serve with rice bhakri.

Serves 8

ROASTED WHOLE ONION

Cut off top and bottom of 1 large unpeeled onion and brush with a few drops of oil. Using tongs, roast over an open flame till the peel is charred and onion softens. Discard peel and use as required. You can roast whole unpeeled garlic bulbs the same way.

ROASTED DRIED COCONUT HALVES

Hold each dried coconut half with tongs over an open flame and roast, turning to brown on all sides. Scrape off blackened surface and use as required.

KOMBDICHE LAPCHAP

Chicken in a Thick Coconut Curry

I like to describe lapchap, which is a thick, robust curry, as the odd one out amongst Kolhapur's signature thin broth-like gravies. Though in Kolhapur I have always encountered this dish with chicken, I have tried preparing it with fish and mutton, and the results are just as delightful.

Ingredients

4 tablespoons oil
4 onions, finely chopped
2 country chickens, cut into 10-12 pieces each
1 cup yoghurt, whisked
Salt
Chopped coriander leaves, to garnish

Spice paste
20 dried red Kashmiri chillies
1½ teaspoons poppy seeds
1½ tablespoons dried lichen
5 (2.5-cm) cinnamon sticks
1½ teaspoons cumin seeds
1 tablespoon coriander seeds
1½ teaspoons black cumin seeds
1 tablespoon sesame seeds
1 tablespoon fennel seeds
10 cloves
8 green cardamom pods
2 bay leaves

Method

- Dry-roast all the ingredients for the spice paste on a griddle. Cool and grind with a little water to a paste.
- Heat the oil in a pan; add the onions and sauté till golden brown. Add the chicken and sauté for 2 minutes. Add the spice paste and sauté till the oil separates.
- Add the yoghurt, salt and 1 cup water and cook till the chicken is tender and gravy thick.
- Serve hot, garnished with chopped coriander leaves.

Serves 10

MARAL RASSA

MURREL CURRY

This dish can be classified as a shikar dish, cooked with the spoils of a hunt. The snakehead murrel, named for its large head resembling a snake, is a huge fish that was often hunted by Kolhapur royalty. The hunters would gather around a crystal clear shallow water body at dawn and look out for the flash of fins. As the fish came to the surface for a gulp of air, the head was momentarily exposed and a lucky and observant hunter could walk away with a good catch.

Ingredients

SPICE PASTE

2 Roasted Onions (page 42)
2 teaspoons roasted poppy seeds
¼ cup grated dried coconut, roasted
½ cup fresh coriander
2 green chillies

FISH CURRY

1kg snakehead murrel, sliced across the bone
1 tablespoon turmeric powder
Salt
2 tablespoons ginger-garlic paste
3 tablespoons oil
1 tablespoon red chilli powder
1½ teaspoons coriander-cumin powder
1 cup tamarind pulp
Chopped coriander leaves, to garnish

Method

- Grind all the ingredients for the spice paste.
- Marinate the fish slices in a mixture of turmeric, salt and 1 tablespoon ginger-garlic paste.
- Roast the fish on a griddle, or grill on a barbecue, till cooked on both sides.
- Heat the oil in a wok; add the remaining ginger-garlic paste, the spice paste, chilli powder, coriander-cumin powder, tamarind pulp and salt. Cook for a few minutes.
- Add the fish and cook on a low heat for 1 minute.
- Garnish with coriander leaves and serve with a salad.

Serves 8

KOLHAPURI DAHI MUTTON

MUTTON COOKED WITH YOGHURT

Yoghurt has a special place in a Kolhapuri kitchen. While it may not be used often in cooking, yoghurt is a staple at every meal. Kolhapuris are justifiably proud of the thick, creamy yoghurt made from fresh cow or buffalo milk. In this recipe, the amount of yoghurt used is equal to that of meat, thus giving the dish its name.

Ingredients

1kg mutton, cut into 5-cm pieces
1kg yoghurt, whisked
1 tablespoon ginger-garlic paste
Salt
1 tablespoon cumin seeds
5 (2.5-cm) cinnamon sticks
10 cloves
10 green cardamom pods
1½ tablespoons oil
4 onions, finely chopped
1 fresh coconut, grated and ground to paste
5 whole dried red chillies

Method

- Marinate the mutton in a mixture of the yoghurt, ginger-garlic paste and salt for 1 hour.
- Grind the cumin seeds, cinnamon, cloves and cardamoms to a fine powder.
- Heat the oil in a pan; add the onion and sauté till pink. Add the fresh coconut paste and sauté for a few minutes.
- Add the mutton, ground spice mixture and whole red chillies, and cook till the meat is tender and gravy thick.
- Serve hot, garnished with chopped coriander leaves.

Serves 8

HIRWA RASSA

GREEN MUTTON CURRY

As a child, I was completely averse to eating vegetables of any sort and would be quite indignant when I was forced to eat a vegetarian dish. At such times, I would cajole the cook into making this spinach-based curry so as to be able to convince my mother that I was getting my quota of healthy greens.

Ingredients

4 tablespoons oil
4 onions, finely chopped
1 tablespoon ginger-garlic paste
1½ teaspoons coriander powder
1 tablespoon Garam Masala (page 34)
Salt
1kg mutton on the bone, cut into 5-cm pieces
Chopped fresh red chillies, to garnish

SPICE PASTE

½ cup grated fresh coconut, roasted
1 tablespoon roasted poppy seeds
1 tablespoon sesame seeds

SPINACH PASTE

2 cups chopped spinach leaves
1 cup fresh coriander
15 green chillies

Method

- For the spice paste, grind the coconut, poppy seeds and sesame seeds to a fine paste.
- For the spinach paste, blend all the ingredients in a blender to make a smooth purée.
- Heat the oil in a pan; add the onions and sauté till pink. Add the ginger-garlic paste, coriander powder, garam masala, salt, spice paste and spinach paste; stir to mix and sauté till the oil separates.
- Add the mutton and sauté for 5 minutes till the spices coat the meat. Add 2 cups water and cook on a low heat till the mutton is tender.
- Garnish with chopped fresh red chillies and serve with steamed rice or bhakri.

Serves 8

MUTTONACHE TAAZE LONCHE

MUTTON COOKED IN PICKLING SPICES

Every region has its own version of 'achaari' meat pickled in spices. The word 'taaze' (fresh) in this dish refers to meat which is boiled rather than roasted or deep-fried before being enrobed in spices. The dish is eaten fresh and tastes best with hot wholewheat rotis.

Ingredients

SPICE POWDER
10 cloves
5 (2.5-cm) cinnamon sticks
1 tablespoon cumin seeds

SPICE PASTE
1 tablespoon poppy seeds
2 teaspoons dried lichen
½ teaspoon cassia buds
2 teaspoons sesame seeds
1 teaspoon black cumin seeds

ROASTED ONION PASTE
1 onion
10 garlic cloves
2.5-cm piece ginger

MUTTON
1kg mutton on the bone, cut into 5-cm pieces
¼ cup chopped ginger
¼ cup chopped garlic
10 green chillies, chopped
1 fresh coconut, grated
4-5 tablespoons oil
1½ teaspoons roasted fenugreek seeds
1 teaspoon husked split mustard seeds
½ teaspoon asafoetida
1 tablespoon coriander seeds
1 tablespoon turmeric powder
Salt
Chopped coriander leaves, to garnish

Method

- Grind the ingredients for the spice powder. Dry-roast the ingredients for the spice paste and grind with a little water to a fine paste. Dry-roast the ingredients for the onion paste and grind to a paste.
- Place the mutton, ginger, garlic, green chillies and grated coconut in a pan with water to cover; cook till the mutton is tender. Drain the excess water.
- Heat the oil in a pan; add the fenugreek seeds, mustard seeds, asafoetida, coriander seeds, and turmeric powder and sauté for a few seconds.
- Add the ground spice powder, spice paste, roasted onion paste and salt; sauté till the oil separates.
- Add the cooked mutton and sauté till the meat is coated with the spices.
- Serve hot, garnished with chopped coriander leaves.

Serves 8

KOLHAPURI MUTTON LONCHE

MUTTON PICKLE

This is traditional travellers' food as the deep-fried meat steeped in spices, with very little extra oil added, keeps well without refrigeration. Back in the day, it was eaten with millet bread and washed down with buttermilk; and in the evening, when the caravan came to a halt, the spice mixture would be ground to a paste to give body and flavour to any curry that was cooked over a campfire. You can substitute the mutton with deep-fried meaty chunks of murrel or boneless chicken.

Ingredients

1kg boneless mutton, cubed
1½ teaspoons turmeric powder
2½ teaspoons red chilli powder
Salt
Oil for deep-frying
1 cup grated dried coconut, dry-roasted
1½ teaspoons sesame seeds, dry-roasted
1½ tablespoons poppy seeds
1 teaspoon turmeric powder
1½ teaspoons red chilli powder
2½ teaspoons Garam Masala (page 34)
2 teaspoons cumin powder
1 teaspoon coriander powder
½ cup sliced garlic
¼ cup chopped ginger
10-15 whole green chillies
1 cup chopped coriander leaves
Juice of 1 lime

Method

- Marinate the meat in a mixture of the turmeric powder, chilli powder and salt for at least 10 minutes.
- Place the meat in a pressure cooker with 2 cups water and cook under pressure till the pressure is released 4 times (4 whistles). When the pressure has reduced, remove the lid and strain the mutton.
- Heat the oil for deep-frying in a wok; add the cooked mutton and fry on medium heat till brown. Remove the mutton with a slotted spoon and drain on absorbent paper.
- Mix together the roasted coconut and sesame seeds, the poppy seeds, turmeric and chilli powders, garam masala, cumin and coriander powders and salt.
- Heat 3 tablespoons oil in a pan; sauté the sliced garlic till brown and remove. To the same pan, add the ginger and sauté till brown and remove. Add the green chillies and coriander to the pan and sauté for a few minutes and remove.
- Place the fried mutton in a bowl; add the roasted coconut mixture, and the fried garlic, ginger, chillies, coriander and lime juice, and toss to mix thoroughly.
- Serve immediately, or store for up to 2 weeks.

Serves 8

NARALI KOMBDI

Chicken in Coconut Milk

This recipe, though simple to put together, has earned me many admirers over the years. No matter what kind of a complex feast I lay out for my guests, they always do the most justice to this comforting dish of tender chicken cooked in fragrant spices and creamy coconut milk.

Ingredients

1kg chicken, cut into 10-12 pieces
1 tablespoon ginger-garlic paste
Salt
2 fresh coconuts, grated
½ cup ghee
4 onions, sliced
4 tablespoons yoghurt
Chopped coriander leaves, to garnish

Spice paste
12 dried red Kashmiri chillies
1 tablespoon coriander seeds
4-5 onions, chopped
1 tablespoon chopped ginger
1 tablespoon chopped garlic

Spice powder
6 green cardamom pods
1½ tablespoons black cumin seeds
4 (2.5-cm) cinnamon sticks
6 black peppercorns
6 cloves

Method

- Marinate the chicken in a mixture of ginger-garlic paste and salt for at least 30 minutes.
- Grind all the ingredients for the spice paste.
- Grind all the ingredients for the spice powder.
- Extract the coconut milk from the grated coconut (see below). Cook in a pan over low heat till it thickens.
- Heat the ghee in a separate pan; add the sliced onions and sauté till pink. Add the marinated chicken and sauté for a few minutes.
- Add the whisked yoghurt, salt and spice paste to the chicken and sauté for a few minutes. Stir in the thickened coconut milk and spice powder.
- Garnish with chopped coriander and serve with wholewheat phulkas.

Serves 8

COCONUT MILK
For 1 cup regular coconut milk, soak 1 cup grated coconut in 1 cup warm water for 10 minutes; blend and strain. For ½ cup thick milk, use ½ cup warm water and 1 cup grated coconut; for 1 cup thin milk, add 1 cup water to solids after extracting thick milk.

PANDHRA RASSA

WHITE MUTTON CURRY

Though Kolhapur is world-renowned for its Pandhra Rassa, few people know that this delicately flavoured dish actually originated in the kitchens of the Gaekwads of Baroda, now in Gujarat State. The Gaekwads make as many as 14 variations of the dish, each with a unique flavour and character. This one is my personal favourite.

To keep the curry creamy white and still have the fiery heat Kolhapuris love, chilli seeds are procured from a grocer who collects the seeds for just such a purpose. The broth is made more flavourful by cooking the meat in a stock made from mutton bones, much like a yakhni, with which this dish shares some similarities.

Ingredients

1½kg boneless mutton, cut into 5-cm cubes
2 cups yoghurt
6 tablespoons oil
2-3 bay leaves
6 onions, finely chopped
1½ tablespoons ginger-garlic paste
100g khoya/mawa
3 cups mutton stock (see note)
1½ cups Coconut Milk (page 54)
Juice of 1 lime
2-3 green chillies, slit
Salt

SPICE PASTE

4 bay leaves
2½ tablespoons dried chilli seeds
2½ tablespoons raw rice
1½ teaspoons poppy seeds
1 tablespoon coriander seeds
1 tablespoon cumin seeds
1 tablespoon black cumin seeds
1½ tablespoons fennel seeds
1½ tablespoons white peppercorns
1½ tablespoons cloves
5 small cinnamon sticks
½ cup cashew nuts
1 tablespoon sesame seeds
6 green cardamom pods
1½ teaspoons mace
A small piece of nutmeg
1½ tablespoons dried lichen
4 star anise

Method

- Combine the mutton and yoghurt in a bowl and set aside for at least 30 minutes.
- Grind all the ingredients for the spice paste to a fine paste.
- Heat the oil in a pan; add the bay leaves and chopped onions and sauté till the onions turn pink. Add the ginger-garlic paste with a little water so that the paste does not burn, and sauté for a minute. Add the spice paste and sauté for 2-3 minutes.
- Add the marinated mutton and khoya and sauté for 5 minutes. Pour in the stock, cover the pan and cook till the mutton is tender.
- Stir in the coconut milk, lime juice, green chillies and salt. Cook for another 2 minutes and remove from heat.
- Garnish with chopped coriander and serve with bhakri.

Note: To make mutton stock, boil mutton bones in water with salt and whole spices like cinnamon, cloves, cardamoms and peppercorns for 10-15 minutes in a pressure cooker. Drain and reserve the stock.

Serves 8

TAMBDA RASSA

RED MUTTON CURRY

Tambda means red. This curry gets its fiery colour thanks to the technique used to make the tempering of Byadagi chilli powder that is poured over the meaty rassa or curry. Not only does this hearty broth make the taste buds tingle, but in Kolhapur it is also popular as a most delicious cure for colds.

Ingredients

6 tablespoons oil
4 bay leaves
6 onions, finely chopped
1 tablespoon turmeric powder
1½ tablespoons ginger-garlic paste
2 tablespoons Kanda-Lasun Masala (page 25)
1½kg mutton on the bone, cut into 5-cm pieces
100g mutton fat, chopped
Juice of 1 lime
Salt
Chopped coriander, to garnish

SPICE PASTE
20 dried red Byadagi chillies
1 large Roasted Onion (page 42)
1 tablespoon coriander seeds
1 tablespoon cumin seeds
1 tablespoon black cumin seeds
1½ tablespoons fennel seeds
1½ tablespoons black peppercorns
1½ tablespoons cloves
5 (2.5-cm) cinnamon sticks
1 tablespoon sesame seeds
6 green cardamom pods
6 black cardamom pods
1½ teaspoons mace
A small piece of nutmeg
1½ tablespoons dried lichen
4 star anise
1½ teaspoons poppy seeds, roasted
2½ tablespoons grated dried coconut

Method

- For the spice paste, in a frying pan, dry-roast each of the ingredients separately (except roasted poppy seeds and coconut) till fragrant. Cool and grind to a paste.
- Heat the oil in a pan; add the bay leaves and chopped onions and sauté till the onions turn golden brown.
- Add the turmeric powder and ginger-garlic paste with a little water so that the paste does not burn. Add the kanda-lasun masala and sauté for 2-3 minutes.
- Add the mutton and the fat, and sauté for 5 minutes. Pour in 2 cups boiling water, cover the pan and cook on low heat till the mutton is half cooked.
- Stir in the spice paste, lime juice and salt; cover the pan and cook till the mutton is tender. If the gravy is too thick add a little water and bring to a boil.
- Garnish with chopped coriander leaves and serve hot with rice or bhakri.

Serves 10

BHARLELI KOMBDI

STUFFED POT ROAST CHICKEN

Whenever I have cooked this dish for a party, people have mistaken it to be my version of Awadhi murgh mussallam. Though quite similar in concept, the difference between the two is that here, the chicken is stuffed and cooked in a wok (kadhai), and the pan juices are used to make the gravy; whereas in the former, the dish is baked.

Ingredients

2 (1.2 kg each) whole chickens
1½ teaspoons ginger-garlic paste
Salt
½ cup ghee

SPICE PASTE
2 tablespoons coriander seeds
2 tablespoons grated dried coconut
½ cup almonds
1½ tablespoons fennel seeds
A small piece of nutmeg
1½ tablespoons black cumin seeds

STUFFING
4-5 tablespoons oil
4-5 onions, sliced
1 fresh coconut, grated
4 (2.5-cm) cinnamon sticks
10 cloves
10 peppercorns
1 teaspoon coriander powder
Juice of 1 lime
5 green chillies, chopped

GRAVY
2 tablespoons ghee
4 onions, finely chopped
4-5 green cardamom pods
8 cloves
3 (2.5-cm) cinnamon sticks
1 cup yoghurt

TO SERVE
Fresh onion, tomato and cucumber salad

Serves 10

Method

- Make small gashes in the chickens and rub all over with the ginger-garlic paste and salt. Leave to marinate for 30 minutes.
- Finely grind all the ingredients for the spice paste; set aside.
- For the stuffing, heat 3 tablespoons oil in a frying pan; sauté the sliced onions till brown; remove and set aside. Add the remaining oil to the pan and sauté the coconut till it turns brown. Coarsely grind the coconut. Grind the cinnamon, cloves and peppercorns to a fine powder.
- In a bowl, combine the fried onions, ground coconut, powdered spices, coriander powder, lime juice, green chillies and salt.
- Stuff the cavities of the chickens with the coconut mixture and stitch the openings up with kitchen twine to seal.
- Heat ½ cup ghee in a large frying pan; add the chickens, one at a time, and sauté till brown on all sides. Remove and set aside.
- For the gravy, heat the ghee in a pan or wok large enough to hold both the chickens. Add the chopped onion and sauté till golden brown. Add the cardamoms, cloves and cinnamon and sauté till fragrant.
- Add the spice paste along with the whisked yoghurt, stir well and cook to make a thick gravy.
- Add the browned chickens with their pan juices, and simmer, covered, for 15 minutes or till tender, turning the chickens over in between to coat with the gravy.
- Serve hot with a fresh cucumber, tomato and onion salad on the side.

KHIMYACHI PARSUNDI

EGGS ON MINCED MUTTON

The elder daughter of Chhatrapati Shahu Maharaj (the first Maharaja of the Princely State of Kolhapur) was married to the King of Dewas (now in Madhya Pradesh). Being fond of cooking, she learned many recipes and would recreate them for her father whenever she visited him. The dried fruit speaks of the upper class origins of the dish, as they were beyond the reach of the common man. The dish shares interesting similarities with the Bohra Lagan Ni Seekh which is also minced meat cooked in a shallow frying pan and topped with eggs.

Ingredients

½ cup roasted poppy seeds
½ cup grated coconut
5 tablespoons ghee
6 onions, finely chopped
1 tablespoon ginger-garlic paste
1½ cup yoghurt, whisked
10 green chillies, finely chopped
1 cup fresh coriander, finely chopped
½ cup almonds, sliced
¼ cup raisins, soaked
¼ cup sultanas, soaked
Juice of 1 lime
Salt
2½ tablespoons Garam Masala (page 34)
1½ tablespoons red chilli powder
½ teaspoon turmeric powder
1kg minced goat meat
12 eggs
A big pinch of saffron, soaked in 3 tablespoons warm water
Dahi kanda (salad of yoghurt, sliced onion, chopped green chillies and salt), to serve

Method

- Grind the poppy seeds and coconut with a little water to a paste.
- Heat the ghee in a wide, shallow frying pan. Add the chopped onions and sauté till brown.
- Add the ginger-garlic paste and ground coconut paste and sauté on low heat till the ghee separates. Stir in the whisked yoghurt.
- Add the remaining ingredients (except the minced meat, eggs and saffron), and sauté for 2 minutes. Add the minced meat and cook, covered, till the mince is tender, and the water has dried up. Press the mince down to even the surface.
- Break all the eggs in a bowl and without whisking pour them over the cooked mince so they cover the top evenly. Pour the soaked saffron with the water over the eggs. Cover the pan with a lid and cook till the eggs set.
- Cut in wedges or squares and serve warm with dahi kanda or a salad.

Serves 8

GOLI PULAO

RICE WITH MEATBALLS

This stunning meatball pilaf evokes fun-filled memories of my visits to my grand-aunt, whose old cook would get jumpy whenever I entered the kitchen. I loved this pulao so much that I would request him to cook it every day, and the dear old man would have no choice but to oblige. His reluctance is understandable now, as this pulao must have been tedious to prepare; the meat had to be ground to a fine paste on a stone. However, the extra effort didn't deter him from making it the way I liked it – more meatballs than rice!

Ingredients

1kg long-grained rice
1kg minced mutton
1 tablespoon ginger-garlic paste
Salt
Oil for deep-frying
2-3 bay leaves
½ teaspoon black peppercorns
5-6 cloves
4 onions, sliced
3 tomatoes, chopped
2 green chillies
1 tablespoon ginger-garlic paste
1 tablespoon grated fresh coconut
1 teaspoon turmeric powder
1 teaspoon Garam Masala (page 34)

Method

- Wash the rice, drain and set aside.
- Place the minced mutton in a bowl; add the ginger-garlic paste and salt and mix well. Shape the mixture into 2.5-cm balls.
- Heat the oil in a wok; deep-fry the meatballs till golden brown. Drain on absorbent paper.
- Heat 2-3 tablespoons oil in a thick-bottomed pan. Add the bay leaves, peppercorns, cloves and onions, and sauté till the onions turn golden. Add the tomatoes, green chillies, ginger-garlic paste, coconut and turmeric powder; sauté for few minutes.
- Add the rice and sauté on medium heat for about 7-8 minutes till dry. Add the garam masala and sauté for 2-3 minutes.
- Stir in 1½ litres hot water and salt. Cover the pan with a lid and cook on high heat for about 4-5 minutes. Uncover the pan and stir the rice very carefully, bringing the rice at the bottom to the top. Lower the heat and cook for about 8-10 minutes till the rice is tender.
- Mix the fried meatballs gently into the rice. Cover and cook for another 4 or 5 minutes.
- Serve hot with mutton curry.

Serves 4 to 6

KOLHAPURI BADAK MASALA

SPICY DUCK CURRY

Duck shooting was a popular pastime of the nobility in the old days in Kolhapur. The game birds were brought in and first scrubbed clean with a mixture of lime juice and sorghum flour before being cooked to make this mouth-watering curry. A shot of rum added to the curry gives it an appealing lift.

Ingredients

1 medium-sized duck, cut into large pieces with the skin
2 tablespoons sorghum flour
1 tablespoon vinegar
Salt
Juice of 1 lime
1 teaspoon turmeric powder
2 teaspoons red chilli powder
½ cup oil
15 green chillies
¼ cup peeled and roughly chopped ginger
¼ cup peeled and roughly chopped garlic
1 cup fresh coriander
½ cup grated fresh coconut, roasted
½ cup grated dried coconut, roasted
1 teaspoon mustard seeds
½ teaspoon fenugreek seeds, roasted
7 onions, finely chopped
7 (2.5-cm) cinnamon sticks
10 cloves
4 bay leaves
10 black cardamom pods
2 tablespoons Garam Masala (page 34)
½ teaspoon cumin seed powder
100ml dark rum
1 cup freshly chopped coriander

Method

- Wash the duck and rub all over with a mixture of sorghum flour and vinegar. Rinse the duck well and pat dry. Marinate the duck in a mixture of salt, lime juice, turmeric and chilli powder for 30 minutes.
- Heat the oil in a pan; add the duck and fry till lightly browned on both sides. Remove and set aside.
- To the same pan, add the chillies, ginger, garlic and coriander; sauté till the garlic turns brown. Strain the mixture to remove the excess oil. Reserve the oil.
- Place the fried ingredients in a blender with the roasted fresh and dried coconut, mustard and fenugreek seeds; blend to a fine paste.
- Heat the strained oil in a pan; add the onions and sauté till golden brown. Add the cinnamon, cloves, bay leaves, cardamoms, garam masala, cumin seed powder and the ground paste; sauté for a minute. Stir in the salt and rum and cook till the oil separates.
- Add the chopped coriander and sauté for 1 minute. Add the duck and 1 or 2 cups water. Cook till the duck is tender and the gravy thickens.
- Serve with rice or jowar bhakri.

Serves 4

KOLHAPURI MUTTON SUKKA

MUTTON COATED WITH COCONUT AND SPICES

I was all of 15 when I made this mutton dish for the very first time. My friends and I had gone out for a round of shikar (it was not yet banned then). Our hunt was successful and I eagerly displayed my culinary skills by preparing this dish. I discovered that not only did I enjoy cooking, but I enjoyed playing host so much that inviting people over and treating them to elaborate feasts soon became a hobby!

Ingredients

1kg mutton on the bone, cut into 5-cm pieces, or mutton chops
1 tablespoon ginger-garlic paste
1 tablespoon turmeric powder
1 tablespoon red chilli powder
Salt
4 tablespoons oil
Chopped coriander leaves, to garnish

SPICE PASTE
1 tablespoon oil
1½ teaspoons coriander seeds
6 (2.5-cm) cinnamon sticks
8 black cardamom pods
10 cloves
½ roasted dried coconut (page 42), grated
1 tablespoon poppy seeds, roasted
6 onions, sliced and deep-fried till golden brown

Method

- For the spice paste, heat the oil in a frying pan and sauté the coriander seeds, cinnamon, cardamoms and cloves till fragrant.
- Combine the fried spices, roasted coconut, poppy seeds, and the fried onion; grind to a paste.
- Combine the mutton with the spice paste, ginger-garlic paste, turmeric powder, chilli powder and salt; leave to marinate for 30 minutes.
- Heat the oil in a pan; add the marinated mutton and 1-1½ cups water and cook on a low heat till the mutton is tender, and the gravy has dried up and just coats the meat.
- Garnish with chopped coriander leaves and serve hot with millet flatbreads.

Serves 8

KOLHAPURI METHI MUTTON

MUTTON WITH FENUGREEK LEAVES

In a departure from the usual practice of adding spices to hot oil and waiting for them to sizzle and pop, this recipe calls for mixing together all the ingredients, including the spices and mutton, and cooking them without oil for a few minutes. Oil is only added when the meat begins to release its juices, thus ensuring that the mutton retains its meaty flavour without being overpowered by the spices.

Ingredients

1kg mutton on the bone, cut into 5-cm pieces
2½ tablespoons ginger-garlic paste
5 onions
2½ tablespoons grated dried coconut
1 tablespoon Garam Masala (page 34)
1½ teaspoons coriander powder
1 cup cold-pressed groundnut oil
4 cups fresh fenugreek leaves, ground to a paste
7 green chillies
Salt

Serves 8

Method

- Combine the mutton with 1 tablespoon ginger-garlic paste and leave to marinate for at least 1 hour.
- Grind 3 onions with the remaining 1½ tablespoons ginger-garlic paste; finely chop the remaining onions. Grind the dried coconut with a little water to a paste.
- In a heavy-bottomed pan, combine the marinated mutton, finely chopped onion, garam masala, coriander powder and coconut paste; cook the meat and spices, stirring constantly, for a few minutes.
- Add the oil and sauté till the aroma of the oil disappears. Add the fenugreek paste, green chillies and 2-3 cups water, and cook on a low heat till the mutton is tender and gravy thick.
- Serve hot, sprinkled over with a pinch of garam masala.

KOLHAPURI LAHORI MASALA

QUAIL CURRY

Hunting or shikar was the favourite pastime of the royals and quails were the preferred prey, thanks to them being found in groups of 10 to 12, which were easy to spot from a distance. Indian quails are tiny, but Japanese quails are bigger and have more meat on them. Quail hunting is banned in India, but commercially bred Japanese quail are easily available for consumption.

Ingredients

1kg quail
1 cup yoghurt, whisked
Salt
1½ teaspoons turmeric powder
2 teaspoons red chilli powder
Juice of 1 lime
½ cup oil
8 onions, finely chopped
2 tablespoons ginger-garlic paste
2 cups boiling water

SPICE PASTE
15 dried red Kashmiri chillies
1 cup grated dried coconut
2 teaspoons fennel seeds
2 teaspoons poppy seeds
2 teaspoons sesame seeds
2 teaspoons coriander seeds
1½ teaspoons cumin seeds
1½ teaspoons black cumin seeds
4 (2.5-cm) cinnamon sticks
20 black peppercorns
20 cloves
10 green cardamom pods
10 black cardamom pods
1 teaspoon mace
1 teaspoon grated nutmeg
2 teaspoons dried lichen
5 star anise

Method

- Place the quail in a bowl with the yoghurt, salt, turmeric powder, chilli powder and lime juice; mix well and leave to marinate for 30 minutes.
- For the spice paste, dry-roast the ingredients on a griddle or frying pan till fragrant. Cool and grind with a little water to a fine paste.
- Heat the oil in a pan; add the chopped onions and sauté till golden brown. Add the ginger-garlic paste and sauté for 2 minutes. Add the spice paste and sauté till the oil separates.
- Add the quail with the marinade and the boiling water. Cover tightly with a lid and cook on low heat till tender.
- Serve with rice.

Serves 4

KOLHAPURI KOMBDI DUM PULAO

SLOW-COOKED CHICKEN PULAO

Kolhapur royalty enjoyed 10 signature rice preparations out of which this was one. What makes it unique is the use of khoya that is generally only used in sweets and occasionally in rich curries.

Ingredients

SPICE PASTE
5 green cardamom pods
6 cloves
3 (2.5-cm) cinnamon sticks
1 teaspoon black peppercorns
2 bay leaves
1 teaspoon coriander seeds

CHICKEN
2 cups yoghurt, whisked
2 tablespoons ginger-garlic paste
½ cup chopped fresh coriander
½ cup chopped fresh mint
4 green chillies, finely chopped
6 onions, sliced and deep-fried till golden brown
1 teaspoon nutmeg powder
Salt
1kg chicken, cut into 10-12 pieces
½ cup ghee

RICE
1kg long-grained rice
1½ teaspoons black cumin seeds
4 (2.5-cm) cinnamon sticks
10 cloves
Salt
3 tablespoons khoya/mawa
A pinch of saffron
½ cup melted ghee

Method

- For the spice powder, dry-roast all the spices lightly in a frying pan or griddle. Cool and grind to a fine powder.
- In a bowl, combine the whisked yoghurt, ginger-garlic paste, chopped coriander and chopped mint, green chillies, fried onions, nutmeg and salt to taste. Add the chicken, mix well and leave to marinate for 15 minutes.
- Heat the ghee in a small pan and pour over the marinated chicken. Mix gently and set aside for half an hour.
- Cook the rice with the black cumin, cinnamon, cloves and salt in a pan with plenty of boiling water till half cooked. Drain the water.
- To assemble the pulao, spread half the rice at the bottom of a large heavy-bottomed pan. Spread the chicken on top of the rice. Sprinkle with the crumbled khoya and saffron. Spread the rest of the rice on top. Pour the melted ghee over the rice. Cover the pan tightly and cook on low heat for 45 minutes.
- Serve with mixed vegetable raita and fried papad.

Serves 4 to 6

GAOTHI KOMBDI RASSA

COUNTRY CHICKEN CURRY

In Kolhapur, this dish is available locally as 'khadki rassa,' the word khadki being the term used for chicken in the local dialect. For this curry, a whole cleaned native breed or country chicken is roasted over a bonfire, till the natural oils caramelise the skin. This process gives the chicken a unique texture and smoky flavour.

Ingredients

1kg country chicken, cut into 10-12 pieces
2 teaspoons red chilli powder
1 teaspoon turmeric powder
Salt
Juice of 1 lime
1½ cups grated fresh coconut
1 cup finely chopped fresh coriander
4-5 green chillies, chopped
1 tomato, finely chopped
4 tablespoons oil
6 onions, finely chopped
20 dried red Kashmiri chillies, soaked and ground to a paste
1½ teaspoons Garam Masala (page 34)
1½ teaspoons Kanda-Lasun Masala (page 25)
1½ teaspoons Goda Masala (page 33)
1 tablespoon ginger-garlic paste
1½ teaspoons coriander powder
1½ teaspoons cumin powder

Method

- Marinate the chicken in a mixture of the chilli powder, turmeric powder, salt and lime juice for 30 minutes.
- Grind the grated coconut, coriander, chillies and tomato to a fine paste.
- Heat the oil in a pan; add the chopped onions and sauté till brown. Add the red chilli paste, garam masala, kanda-lasun masala, goda masala, ginger-garlic paste, coriander powder, cumin powder and salt; sauté till the oil separates.
- Add the marinated chicken and 2-3 cups water to make a thin gravy. Cook till the chicken is tender and serve hot with rice.

Serves 4

MUNDI RASSA

Goat's Head Curry

A delicious curry, spicy enough to make smoke emanate from your ears, mundi rassa is a hot – literally – favourite of diehard meat aficionados. Though most fans like to eat it with rice, I prefer hot rice bhakris and thecha (a spicy chutney of green chillies and garlic) which ramps up the heat even further.

Ingredients

3 tablespoons oil
3 onions, finely chopped
1½ tablespoons ginger-garlic paste
2 teaspoons turmeric powder
1 tablespoon red chilli powder
Salt to taste
2 goat heads, cut into pieces

Spice paste

1 tablespoon poppy seeds
1½ tablespoons sesame seeds
1½ tablespoons coriander seeds
1½ teaspoons cumin seeds
12 dried red chillies
½ dried coconut, grated
3 Roasted Onions (page 42)
1 tablespoon Garam Masala (page 34)
1 tablespoons Kanda-Lasun Masala (page 25)
2 tablespoons oil

Method

- Heat the oil in a thick-bottomed pan; add the chopped onions and sauté till golden brown. Add the ginger-garlic paste, turmeric powder, chilli powder and salt, and sauté for a minute.
- Add the chopped goat's heads and sauté on high heat for a minute. Add 1 litre water, and bring to a boil. Lower the heat and simmer for 45 minutes to an hour till the meat is tender.
- In the meanwhile, make the spice paste: dry-roast the poppy seeds, sesame seeds, coriander seeds, cumin seeds, red chillies and coconut, till the coconut changes colour. Grind all the ingredients to a fine paste with the roasted onion, garam masala and kanda-lasun masala.
- Heat the oil in a pan; add the spice paste and sauté till the oil separates. Add the cooked goat heads and cook for 10 minutes until the gravy is thick.
- Serve hot with rice bhakri or steamed rice.

Serves 6

Pathare Prabhu

PATHARE PRABHU MASALA

PATHARE PRABHU MUTTON PULAO

PATHARE PRABHU KOMBDI MASALA

KOLAMBICHE KHADAKLE

PATHARE PRABHU MUTTON MASALA

PATHARE PRABHU KOLAMBI MASALA

It is not surprising that a community with such a rich tradition of cultural excellence, and so many legal and academic luminaries and fierce champions of social reform and justice, should have a cuisine that is as vibrant as it is feisty.

The Pathare Prabhus are believed to be descendants of King Ashwapati who reigned in Nepal around the seventh century BCE. They seem to have dispersed as a community all over north India, including Marwar in Rajputana (now Rajasthan) and Patan in Gujarat. In the late thirteenth century, many members of the community travelled with Raja Bhimdev, a Pathare Prabhu, who set up his court at Mahikavati (Mahim) in Mumbai, and settled there. Raja Bhimdev is credited with building the Prabhadevi temple dedicated to goddess Prabhavati, one of the principal deities of the community.

As in all coastal communities, the Pathare Prabhu diet is largely non-vegetarian, comprising mainly fish and seafood cooked with fresh coconut and coconut milk. They often joke that there is no such thing as a vegetarian dish – their vegetables must contain a little dried or fresh fish. Mutton and chicken are reserved for high days and holidays and cooked with the same spices in rich red curries.

Belying the appearance of their dishes, theirs is a quick and uncomplicated method of cooking; a few ingredients tossed into a pan with their signature 'Parbhi' masala and freshly grated coconut. Coconut milk or 'shire' is a particular favourite with coconut milk curries forming an integral part of a meal, eaten with steaming hot rice or chapattis.

Pathare Prabhu food may be simple, but rich it certainly is; the flaming red curries are covered with a glossy slick of pure groundnut oil or ghee. Dried fruit and nuts are added to many of their dishes especially desserts, prepared with only the best quality ingredients.

I feel completely at home in the company of my Pathare Prabhu friends and happy to count myself as a true 'sokaji,' the Pathare Prabhu epithet for lovers of good food and all the good things in life.

PATHARE PRABHU MASALA

PATHARE PRABHU SPICE MIX

This is the go-to spice blend for most Pathare Prabhu dishes. It adds that signature flavour that immediately identifies it as being from a Pathare Prabhu kitchen. As with all regional and community spice mixes, a year's supply is ground and bottled and always kept close at hand to spice up vegetable, fish and meat dishes.

Ingredients

10 dried red chillies
2 tablespoons coriander seeds
1 tablespoon cumin seeds
1½ teaspoons wheat grains
1½ teaspoons split Bengal gram
1 teaspoon fenugreek seeds
½ teaspoon black peppercorns
1½ teaspoons turmeric powder
A pinch of asafoetida

Method

- Dry-roast all the spices, except the turmeric and asafoetida, in a frying pan or griddle till fragrant.
- Cool and grind to a fine powder.
- Mix in the turmeric and asafoetida and store in an airtight jar.

Makes ¾ cup

PATHARE PRABHU MUTTON PULAO

SPICED RICE WITH MUTTON AND EGGS

This recipe comes from my grand-aunt's handwritten notebook of recipes that she enthusiastically collected during her lifetime. One could call this a distant relative of yakhni pulao where meat is boiled with ginger and garlic. The only difference is that yakhni uses mainly white ingredients to maintain the creamy colour, whereas this pulao uses red chilli and ground spices which give it a rich hue.

Ingredients

SPICE POWDER
10 cloves
10 (2.5-cm) cinnamon sticks
10 cardamoms
1½ teaspoons black cumin seeds

PULAO.
1kg long-grained rice
1kg mutton on the bone cut into 5-cm pieces
2 tablespoons ginger-garlic paste
Salt
½ cup ghee
1 cup cashew nuts
6 medium potatoes, parboiled, peeled and cut in quarters
1 tablespoon cumin seeds
10 peppercorns
7 (2.5-cm) cinnamon sticks
10 cloves
10 green cardamom pods
6 medium onions, finely chopped
8 green chillies, slit
1 tablespoon red chilli powder
1 cup yoghurt, whisked
6 hard-boiled eggs, peeled and cut in half

Method

- For the spice powder, grind the ingredients to a fine powder.
- Soak the rice in water for 45 minutes.
- Combine the mutton, ginger-garlic paste and salt and place in a pan. Add water and cover it. Cook till the mutton is tender. Drain and reserve the stock.
- Heat the ghee in a heavy-bottomed pan; fry the cashew nuts till golden brown. Remove with a slotted spoon and set aside.
- To the same pan, add the potatoes and fry till golden brown on all sides. Remove and set aside.
- Add the whole spices to the pan and sauté till fragrant. Add the chopped onion and sauté till golden brown. Add the green chillies, chilli powder and ground spice powder; sauté for a minute.
- Add the rice, yoghurt, salt and 2 litres water including the reserved stock, stir to mix and bring to a boil. Lower the heat and cook, covered, till the rice is half cooked.
- Add the mutton, cashew nuts and potatoes and stir gently to mix. Seal the pan with a tight-fitting lid and cook on low heat till the rice is tender.
- Serve on a platter with the boiled egg halves arranged on top.

Serves 8

PATHARE PRABHU KOMBDI MASALA

COUNTRY CHICKEN CURRY

When it comes to country chickens, there is a way of selecting the perfect chicken for your dish. Remember the mantra; check the legs. The legs of the chicken should be smooth, not scaly. The smoother the legs, the younger and more tender the chicken, and the faster it cooks.

Ingredients

1kg country chicken, cut into 10-12 pieces
2 tablespoons ginger-garlic paste
1 teaspoon turmeric powder
2 tablespoons yoghurt
4 tablespoons oil
2 (2.5-cm) cinnamon sticks
8 cloves
3 green cardamoms
2 large onions, ground to a paste
1½ tablespoons Pathare Prabhu Masala (page 81)
2½ tablespoons red chilli powder
1½ teaspoons coriander powder
3 medium tomatoes, puréed
2 large pinches dried fenugreek leaves
Salt
1½ teaspoons sugar
1 tablespoon cream
1 tablespoon ghee
Chopped coriander leaves, to garnish

Method

- Marinate the chicken in a mixture of half the ginger-garlic paste, the turmeric powder and yoghurt for 30 minutes.
- Heat the oil in a pan; add the cinnamon, cloves and cardamom and sauté till fragrant. Add the onion paste and sauté till the onion turns brown.
- Add the remaining ginger-garlic paste, the Pathare Prabhu masala, chilli powder and coriander powder; sauté for a minute. Add the tomato purée and sauté for a couple of minutes.
- Add the marinated chicken, dried fenugreek leaves, salt, sugar and 2 cups water and cook till the chicken is tender and gravy thick.
- Stir in the cream and ghee, and cook on a low heat for 2 minutes.
- Garnish with coriander leaves and serve hot with phulkas.

Serves 6

KOLAMBICHE KHADAKLE

Quick Prawn Curry with Garlic

This recipe was given to my grand-aunt by her best friend who was from the Pathare Prabhu community. This is one of those dishes that can be turned out in a flash for unexpected guests, or just on a whim.

Ingredients

4 tablespoons oil
1 tablespoon garlic paste
1 tablespoon red chilli powder
1 tablespoon Prathare Prabhu Masala (page 81)
1 teaspoon turmeric powder
¼ teaspoon asafoetida
15 medium-sized prawns, shelled and deveined
Salt
Coriander leaves, to garnish

Method

- Heat the oil in a wok; add the garlic paste, chilli powder, Pathare Prabhu masala, turmeric and asafoetida; sauté for half a minute.
- Add the prawns, salt and a little water and cook for 3 minutes till the prawns are just cooked.
- Serve hot, garnished with coriander leaves.

Serves 6

PATHARE PRABHU MUTTON MASALA

MUTTON CURRY WITH POTATOES

What I love about this recipe is that it uses potatoes with their skins intact. The concept of peelers, even in this day and age, has not entered rural Maharashtrian kitchens. Wherever possible, vegetables and even fruits, are used with their peels. Not only does this add flavour to the curry, it also increases its nutritive value thanks to the minerals in the peels.

Ingredients

4 tablespoons oil
12 black peppercorns
4 cloves
2 (2.5-cm) cinnamon sticks
3 green cardamom pods
1 tablespoon coriander seeds
10 dried red Kashmiri chillies
½ dried coconut, grated
1 onion, finely chopped
1½ tablespoons ginger-garlic paste
1 tablespoon Pathare Prabhu Masala (page 81)
1 teaspoon turmeric powder
½ kg mutton on the bone, cut into 5-cm pieces
Salt
4 medium unpeeled potatoes, cut in half
2 tablespoons ghee
Chopped coriander leaves, to garnish

Method

- Heat 2 tablespoons oil in a frying pan or griddle; add the peppercorns, cloves, cinnamon, cardamoms, coriander seeds, chillies and grated dried coconut and sauté till fragrant. Cool and grind to a paste.
- Heat the remaining oil in a pan; add the chopped onion and sauté till golden brown.
- Add the ginger-garlic paste and sauté for a minute. Add the spice paste, Pathare Prabhu masala and turmeric, and sauté for half a minute.
- Add the mutton and salt and sauté till the meat is coated with the spices.
- Add 1 cup water and cook, covered with a tight fitting lid, till the mutton is half done. Add the potatoes and cook till the mutton and potatoes are tender and the gravy is thick.
- Stir in the ghee and serve hot, garnished with chopped coriander leaves.

Serves 4

PATHARE PRABHU KOLAMBI MASALA

PRAWN CURRY WITH COCONUT MILK

This coconut milk curry has two versions: a thin version and a thicker one made by adding rice flour to thicken the curry and to prevent the coconut milk from curdling. The thicker version is more popular as its velvety texture goes perfectly with rice as well as bhakri or pav.

Ingredients

1 coconut, grated
1½ teaspoons cumin seeds
½ tablespoon fenugreek seeds
1 tablespoon Pathare Prabhu Masala (page 81)
1½ teaspoons red chilli powder
1½ teaspoons turmeric powder
½ cup tamarind pulp
1½ teaspoons rice flour
4 tablespoons ghee
4 onions, finely chopped
30 medium prawns, peeled and deveined
Salt
1½ teaspoons sugar

Method

- Grind together half the grated coconut, the cumin seeds, fenugreek seeds, Pathare Prabhu masala, chilli and turmeric powders with a little water to a fine paste.
- Grind the remaining grated coconut in 1 cup warm water and strain to extract thick coconut milk. Set aside. Grind the coconut residue again with 1 cup warm water and strain to extract thin coconut milk.
- Combine the tamarind pulp and thin coconut milk; stir in the rice flour till smooth.
- Heat the ghee in a pan; add the chopped onions and fry till golden brown. Add the spice paste and sauté till the ghee separates.
- Add the prawns, tamarind-coconut milk mixture, salt and sugar, and cook for 3 minutes. Stir in the thick coconut milk and bring to a gentle boil.
- Remove immediately from heat and serve with bhakri or steamed rice.

Serves 8

Koli

To think there was a time when all the seven islands that made up Mumbai were just koliwadas! The Kolis were the original inhabitants of the islands and lived in a virtual paradise, living off the land and sea before migration, colonisation, and subsequent urbanisation changed their way of life forever. Today, 'koliwadas' are small pockets of Koli habitation usually along Mumbai's coast, within which the community tries almost in vain to preserve its identity in the face of relentless change.

The Kolis have contributed much to Mumbai in addition to names: the city itself is named for the Koli goddess Mumbadevi, and Colaba, one of the most well-known localities in south Mumbai, is a distorted version of Kolbhat or Koli estate.

Koli music, dance, dress and jewellery are a part of the city's cultural panorama, but what Kolis are best known for is seafood. Not only are they native fisher folk who have been harvesting the seas around Mumbai for centuries, but their traditional seafood dishes are the stuff of legend.

I have never been able to pass up an invitation to a Koli meal. The fish is always tail-flapping fresh, the prawns leaping in the basket and the crab sidling slyly away from the cooking pot. The simplest daily meal of rice, ambat (fish curry) with a piece of fried fish or stir-fried prawns is like a feast. Like all seaside communities, they use plenty of coconut, both fresh and dried, which gives the food that special flavour of the coast. Every Koli kitchen has a large barni (ceramic jar) of its special Koli masala or kala masala which is the family secret spice blend. It is a versatile blend that is added in varying proportions to fish, vegetable, lentil, chicken and meat dishes, the latter reserved for feast days and special celebrations. I must confess that I am yet to eat a purely vegetarian Koli dish: like many staunchly non-vegetarian food lovers, they somehow manage to slip in a little extra 'flavour' into vegetarian dishes.

This is where dried fish and prawns play a huge part in Koli cooking. Khar-Danda, a suburb in northwest Mumbai, has been made famous by photographs of rows of bombil (Bombay duck) hanging out to dry in preparation for the monsoons when all fishing is suspended. Whole or sliced fish and prawns are pickled in spices or salted and dried, creating a delicious array of rainy day options.

The monsoons are when the Kolis are able to take a break from fishing to repair their nets and boats before the fishing season starts. They know only too well the dangers of an unforgiving sea, so prayers and worship of sea gods and goddesses are rituals that every Koli fisherman will perform before he sets out to sea. As the monsoons begin to wane, Kolis celebrate Narali Purnima by offering coconuts to lord Varuna and distributing them to friends and neighbours. Soon the winds begin to change and the seas become more gentle. It is time for the Kolis to set sail and begin fishing again.

KOLI MASALA

Koli Spice Mix

An aromatic, pungent spice blend, Koli masala is the mainstay of a Koli kitchen. It provides heat and flavour to a dish depending on the quantity used. The blend is particularly crafted to complement all types of fish and seafood which is the predominant food of this fishing community.

Ingredients

200g dried red Kashmiri chillies
¼ cup coriander seeds
2 tablespoons cumin seeds
1½ tablespoons black peppercorns
1 tablespoon poppy seeds
1 tablespoon sesame seeds
1 tablespoon green cardamom pods
6 bay leaves
6 black cardamom pods
6.25-cm cinnamon stick
2½ teaspoons cloves
1 small piece of turmeric root
2 star anise
1½ teaspoons tirphal/teppal
1 teaspoon mustard seeds
1 teaspoon black cumin seeds
1 teaspoon dried lichen
¾ teaspoon asafoetida
½ teaspoon fennel seeds
½ teaspoon cassia buds
½ teaspoon grated nutmeg
½ teaspoon allspice
½ teaspoon dried mugwort

Method

- Dry-roast the spices on a hot griddle or frying pan till fragrant.
- Cool and grind together to a powder.
- Store in an airtight container.

Makes about 2 cups

KOLI MUTTON MASALA

MUTTON CURRY WITH ROASTED COCONUT

A rough version of this recipe was given to me by a friend who described the method and listed the ingredients. He, however, did not divulge the proportions. But when he brought over some of the dish for me to taste, I used reverse engineering and figured out the details for myself!

Ingredients

4 tablespoons oil
5 onions, finely chopped
1½ tablespoons ginger-garlic-green chilli paste
1 teaspoon turmeric powder
2 tablespoons Koli Masala (page 94)
½ cup grated dried coconut, roasted and ground to paste
1kg mutton on the bone, cut into 5-cm pieces
1 tablespoon Garam Masala (page 34)
Salt
Coriander leaves, to garnish (optional)

Method

- Heat the oil in a pan; add the chopped onions and sauté till golden brown. Add the ginger-garlic-green chilli paste, turmeric, Koli masala and dried coconut; sauté for a few minutes.
- Add the mutton and sauté till coated with the spices. Stir in 4 cups water and cook till the mutton is half done.
- Add the garam masala and salt, and cook till the mutton is tender.
- Garnish with coriander leaves and serve with rice.

Serves 8

NAVSACHA KOMBDA

Smoked Chicken Curry

This dish was traditionally made on the day of a Koli wedding, or the day after, when the bridal couple visited a temple to seek the Almighty's blessings. A hen or rooster was sacrificed and this curry made from the meat in fulfillment of a vow (navas) taken before the deity. The curry was usually cooked on the temple premises itself and the first portion offered to the deity.

Ingredients

1kg chicken, cut into 8-12 pieces
3 tablespoons oil
4 onions, finely chopped
2 bay leaves
4 black cardamom pods
1½ teaspoons cumin seeds
1 cup roasted fresh coconut paste
1 tablespoon ginger-garlic paste
2 tablespoons Koli Masala (page 94)
1 tablespoon Garam Masala (page 34)
2-3 unpeeled potatoes, parboiled and quartered
Salt
A piece of coal for smoking
Chopped coriander leaves, to garnish

Method

- Dry-roast the chicken pieces in a frying pan or in an oven till half cooked; set aside.
- Heat the oil in a pan; add the chopped onions, bay leaves, cardamoms and cumin seeds; sauté till the onions turn brown. Add the coconut paste, ginger-garlic paste, Koli masala and garam masala and sauté for a few minutes.
- Add the potatoes and chicken and stir to coat with the spices. Add 2 cups water and salt, and cook till the chicken is tender.
- Heat the coal on an open flame till red hot and place it in a small heatproof bowl. Place the bowl in the pan with the chicken and cover with a lid for 5 minutes to flavour the chicken.
- Serve hot, garnished with chopped coriander leaves.

Serves 8

KHAADI MUTTON

KOLI SPECIAL MUTTON CURRY

This mutton dish is on many celebratory menus of the Koli community. The Kolis, not surprisingly, love seafood, but they also enjoy meat, especially on special occasions. My beloved Laxman Mama, my constant companion through my childhood and teens, would often request the cook to make this dish and the cook would always oblige; after all, he had learned it from Laxman Mama himself!

Ingredients

1kg mutton on the bone, cut into 5-cm pieces
1 tablespoon turmeric powder
6 tablespoons oil
2 Roasted Coconut halves (page 42)
5 onions, finely chopped
4 (2.5-cm) cinnamon sticks
8 cloves
2 bay leaves
6 green cardamom pods
½ teaspoons asafoetida
1 tablespoon ginger-garlic paste
1½ tablespoons chilli powder
1½ tablespoons Garam Masala (page 34)
Salt
Chopped coriander leaves, to garnish

Method

- Marinate the mutton in a mixture of turmeric and 2 tablespoons oil.
- Chop the roasted coconut into pieces and grind to a paste.
- Heat the remaining 4 tablespoons oil in a pan; add the finely chopped onions and sauté till brown. Add the cinnamon, cloves, bay leaves and cardamoms and sauté till fragrant.
- Add the asafoetida, ginger-garlic paste, chilli powder, garam masala powder and roasted coconut paste. Sauté till the oil separates from the gravy.
- Add the mutton and salt, and sauté till the spices coat the meat. Add 3 cups water and cook till the mutton is tender and gravy thick.
- Serve hot, garnished with chopped coriander leaves.

Serves 8

TEESRYACHI AMTI

CLAM CURRY WITH DRUMSTICK PURÉE

The speciality of this recipe is the addition of drumstick pulp and tender leaves of the drumstick tree, which give it a very unique aroma and flavour. Traditionally, the curry is a thin one, but you may add a little rice flour paste to thicken it.

Ingredients

4 cups (about 50) whole clams, scrubbed well
Salt
3 large drumsticks pods
1 cup drumstick leaves
4 tablespoons oil
1 teaspoon mustard seeds
3 sprigs curry leaves
1½ teaspoons garlic paste
1 cup Browned Onion Paste*
1 teaspoon green chilli paste, or to taste
1 cup roasted fresh coconut paste
1½ teaspoons Garam Masala (page 34)
1½ teaspoons Koli Masala (page 94)
1 teaspoon turmeric powder
1½ teaspoons red chilli powder
1½ teaspoons pepper powder
½ teaspoon cumin powder
½ cup tamarind pulp
Chopped coriander leaves, to garnish

Method

- Place the clams, a little salt and 1½ cups water in a pan and bring to boil. As soon as the clams open, remove from heat. Drain and reserve 1 cup stock. Reserve the bottom half shell with the clam attached, and discard the top shell. Discard any unopened clams.
- Cut the drumsticks into 5-cm pieces and cook in boiling water till soft and tender. Scoop out the pulp and purée in a blender. Separately purée the drumstick leaves in a blender and set aside.
- Heat the oil in a pan; add the mustard seeds, curry leaves and garlic paste, and sauté for a minute. Add the rest of the spice pastes and powders, the puréed drumstick pulp and leaves, and the tamarind pulp and stir well to mix.
- Add the clams and the reserved clam stock and cook for 10 minutes till the curry has thickened slightly.
- Sprinkle coriander leaves over the curry and serve hot with steamed rice.

Serves 4

*BROWNED ONION PASTE

Brown 2 cups sliced onions in 3 tbsp oil. Drain and grind to a thick paste. Makes 1 cup

KOLI KOLAMBI PULAO

Prawn Pulao

Another recipe from my grand-aunt's collection, this pulao is traditionally made using Koli masala with some roasted and ground allspice added to it. Sometimes, though, I like to substitute it with East Indian Bottle Masala, which is just as spicy and just as robust, but still gives the pulao a special zing.

Ingredients

½kg basmati rice
4 tablespoons oil
3 onions, finely chopped
3 bay leaves
2 tablespoons Hirwa Watan (page 38)
1 cup fresh tomato purée
1½ tablespoons Koli Masala (page 94)
1 tablespoon Garam Masala (page 34)
1 teaspoon turmeric powder
1kg peeled and deveined prawns
Salt
Dahi Kanda (page 63), to serve

Method

- Boil the rice in plenty of salted water till half cooked. Drain and set aside to cool.
- Heat the oil in a pan; add the finely chopped onions, bay leaves, hirwa watan, tomato purée, Koli masala, garam masala and turmeric powder and sauté for 4-5 minutes.
- Add the prawns and salt, stir to mix well and cook for 2-3 minutes.
- Spread the partially cooked rice over the prawns, cover the pan tightly and cook on very low heat till the rice is tender.
- Serve hot with dahi kanda.

Serves 6

SHEVAND KOLI MASALA

LOBSTER WITH KOLI SPICES AND GREEN MANGO

I came across this dish in the most unlikely place. I was on my way to Chiplun and had just passed Velneshwar when I happened to spot a toddy tapper making his way up a palm tree. Fascinated, I stopped to watch and ended up befriending him. At lunchtime, he opened his tiffin box to reveal this gem of a dish: lobster cooked in Koli masala, with roasted ground coconut and unripe mango. You can grind the paste as coarsely or as fine as you prefer, though I would recommend leaving it a little coarse for that lovely texture.

Ingredients

2 large lobsters
6 tablespoons oil
8 onions, finely chopped
1 tablespoon ginger-garlic paste
1-2 teaspoons green chilli paste
4 tomatoes, chopped
1 tablespoon Koli Masala (page 94)
1½ teaspoons Garam Masala (page 34)
1½ teaspoons turmeric powder
1½ tablespoons red chilli powder
1 unripe green mango, peeled and grated
Salt
Green mango slices, to garnish (optional)

Method

- Crack the lobsters and remove the meat. Chop the meat in chunks and set aside; reserve the lobster heads and shells.
- Heat 4 tablespoons oil in a pan; add the chopped onions and sauté till brown. Add the ginger-garlic paste and green chilli paste and sauté for a few seconds.
- Add the chopped tomatoes, Koli masala, garam masala, turmeric powder, chilli powder, grated mango and salt. Mix well and cook, stirring occasionally, till the oil separates.
- Add the lobster heads and shells and 2 cups water and bring to a boil. Cook till the gravy reduces by half. Remove from heat and strain the gravy through a sieve into a bowl.
- Heat the remaining oil in a pan; add the lobster meat and cook on high heat for a few minutes. Add the strained gravy and cook till the lobster is tender and gravy thick.
- Serve hot, garnished with slices of green mango.

Serves 6

MORICHE AMBAT TIKHAT

HOT AND SOUR SHARK CURRY

Milk shark or dog shark is a favourite of Konkan coastal communities. It tastes particularly good when cooked in a hot and sour gravy, which usually means with a lot of chillies and tamarind or kokum to temper the heat. Teamed with steaming hot rice, this dish is perfect for a lazy Sunday lunch followed by a peaceful nap.

Ingredients

6 tablespoons oil
3 onions, sliced
4 tomatoes, chopped
1 tablespoon sugar
Salt
1½ tablespoons vinegar
2½ tablespoons tamarind pulp
15 dried red Kashmiri chillies
15 black peppercorns
10 cloves
1 tablespoon cumin seeds
5 (2.5-cm) cinnamon sticks
3 tablespoons Hirwa Watan (page 38)
1½ teaspoons turmeric powder
2 tablespoons red chilli powder
6 kokum rinds
1kg shark, skin removed and cut into 5-cm pieces
Chopped coriander leaves, to garnish (optional)

Method

- Heat 3 tablespoons oil in a wok; add the sliced onions and sauté till brown. Add the tomatoes, sugar and salt, and cook till the tomatoes are soft. Set aside to cool. Grind the cooled mixture to a fine paste with the vinegar, tamarind pulp, chillies, peppercorns, cloves, cumin seeds and cinnamon.
- Heat the remaining oil in a wok; add the hirwa watan, ground onion-tomato paste, turmeric powder, chilli powder and kokum. Sauté till the oil separates.
- Add the fish and 2 cups water. Cook till the fish is tender and the gravy thick.
- Garnish with coriander and serve hot with steamed rice.

Serves 6

Konkan

KHOLAMBA - SARASWAT SAMBHAR MASALA
KONKANI GARAM MASALA
SURMAI TAWA FRY
SARASWAT MUTTON
KOMBDICHI SHAGOTI
SARASWAT BANGDA CURRY
KONKANI KOMBDI SUKKE
SHAHLYATLE MAASE
KOMBDI HIRWA MASALA
PAPLETCHI AMTI
SANGAMESHWARI KOMBDI
BANGDA UDID METHI
TEESRYACHE SUKKE
MORI KHEEMA
BANGDYACHE SUKKE
SHINGADYACHE KALWAN
KOLAMBI BATATA TONDAK
KOLAMBI BIRYANI
PAPLET HIRWA MASALA
MORI LAL MASALA
BHARLELA PAPLET
KOMBDICHA MOTLA
KONKANI KHEKDA MASALA

The Konkan belt is India's own emerald coast – a thin strip of verdant land that stretches along the west coast between the Western Ghats and the Arabian Sea. From Maharashtra to North Kanara, these fertile plains bordered on one side by a bountiful sea, and on the other by hillsides lush with vegetation, give life and livelihoods to many vibrant coastal communities, one of which is the Goud Saraswat Brahmin community.

This community of learned Brahmins from north India once lived on the banks of the mighty Saraswati river till they were forced to migrate when the river began to dry up. Some moved to Kashmir and became Kashmiri Pundits; others went east and set up Brahmin communities in Bengal. A number of them travelled across India to settle in and around Goa as the Goud Saraswats or Dakshinatya Saraswats. It is interesting that these three Saraswat Brahmin communities are the only Brahmins that eat fish, and even meat, the reasons perhaps being the rigours of starvation and forced migration.

With the advent of the Portuguese and the threat of conversion, many Saraswats left Goa and moved further south and north along the Konkan coast and established communities there. Their cuisine in those areas therefore has influences not only of traditional Goan cuisine but also that of North Kanara and Maharashtra. It is important to note that the traditional taste of Goa is not that of vindaloo and sorpotel which is now associated with Goan cuisine, but the more subtle and tempered flavours found in a plate of Saraswat xit-kodi (rice and curry).

Vegetables, seafood and coconuts are at the heart of traditional Saraswat cuisine. On certain days of the week, however, they eat only vegetarian food. Coconut and coconut oil are predominant flavours in their cooking, with tamarind and sometimes kokum, the dried rind of the mangosteen-like fruit, balancing the flavours with a touch of sourness. The predominant flavour, however, comes from the community's generic spice blend called kholamba sambhar masala, that is quite unlike the other sambhar masalas of south Indian cuisines. Kholamba is a mélange of aromatic spices and dried red chillies, usually Byadagi or Kashmiri chillies, which provide more colour than heat. The Saraswats discovered cashew nuts after the Portuguese planted whole hillsides with seeds of the fruit trees they had brought over from their colony in Brazil. They included them in their cooking to add richness and refinement to a dish.

Meat and chicken dishes are reserved for special celebrations and feasts. Shagoti is one of their prized dishes which as Xacuti, a Goan Christian version, has become one of the iconic dishes of Goa. I have included the recipe and many others which you may not find on Konkani menus, but which form a part of one of India's richest hidden culinary treasures.

KHOLAMBA – SARASWAT SAMBHAR MASALA

Saraswat Spice Mix

The cuisine of the Konkani Saraswat community is defined by kholamba masala, which is the community's signature spice blend. I used to find the term 'kholamba' pretty amusing for a spice blend as in Marathi, the word literally translates as 'detained, delayed or stopped.' The term made complete sense when I first made the masala myself and found the task to be quite cumbersome and time consuming, as each ingredient has to be fried separately over a gentle heat.

Ingredients

4 tablespoons oil
250g dried red Kashmiri chillies
2 cups coriander seeds
2 tablespoons split black gram
2 tablespoons split Bengal gram
1½ tablespoons turmeric powder
30 black peppercorns
1½ teaspoons fenugreek seeds
1½ teaspoons asafoetida
1½ tablespoons cumin seeds
1 cup fresh curry leaves

Method

- Heat the oil on a griddle; sauté each ingredient separately.
- Cool and grind to a fine powder.
- Store in an airtight jar with a tight fitting lid.

Makes about 1½ cups

KONKANI GARAM MASALA

KONKANI SPICE MIX

This aromatic spice mix, spiked with the heat of chillies, and redolent of fennel, star anise, cinnamon and tongue-tickling tirphal of the Szechuan pepper family, adds a distinctly Konkan flavour to a dish.

Ingredients

30 Kashmiri chillies
10 black peppercorns
10 cloves
4 bay leaves
4 (2.5-cm) cinnamon sticks
6 star anise
1 tablespoon fennel seeds
6 tirphal/teppal

Method

- Dry-roast each ingredient separately in a frying pan or griddle.
- Cool and grind to a fine powder.
- Store in an airtight jar.

Makes about 1/3 cup

SURMAI TAWA FRY

GRIDDLE-FRIED SEER FISH

This is one of the simplest recipes and is high on my list of 'comfort foods.' Seer fish, also referred to as kingfish, is marinated in spices and fried on a griddle. It is perfect for a quick snack, served with onion rings liberally doused in lime juice, or, as I have recently discovered, with vinegared onions.

Ingredients

FISH
1kg seer fish, sliced across the bone
Salt
Juice of 2 limes
Oil for shallow-frying
Lime wedges and onion rings, to serve (optional)

SPICE PASTE
1 tablespoon red chilli powder
1½ teaspoons black peppercorns
1½ teaspoons cumin seeds
1 tablespoon coriander seeds
2 onions, finely chopped
10 curry leaves
1½ teaspoons finely chopped garlic
A small piece of ginger, chopped

Method

- Wash the fish and rub salt and lime juice on all sides. Set aside for 10 minutes; wash the fish again and drain well.
- Grind all the ingredients for the spice paste.
- Spread the paste all over the fish slices and leave to marinate for at least 1 hour, preferably in the refrigerator.
- Heat the oil in a frying pan or griddle; add the fish slices and fry on both sides till tender and golden brown.
- Serve hot with onion rings and lime wedges on the side.

Serves 6

SARASWAT MUTTON

RICH MUTTON CURRY

This is one for the celebration table. Rich, red and redolent of fragrant spices, including the Saraswat signature kholamba masala, all it needs is steamed rice or a simple pulao to accompany it.

Ingredients

SPICE PASTE
4 tablespoons oil
1 fresh coconut, grated
4 onions, sliced
1½ tablespoons poppy seeds
10 cloves
20 peppercorns

MUTTON CURRY
2 tablespoons oil
2 onions, sliced
6 green cardamom pods
6 cloves
3 bay leaves
½ teaspoon turmeric powder
1 tablespoon red chilli powder
6 tablespoons Hirwa Watan (page 38)
1kg mutton on the bone, cut into 5-cm pieces
1 tablespoon Goda Masala (page 33)
1 tablespoon Kholamba (page 112)
Salt

Method

- For the spice paste, heat the oil in a frying pan or griddle and sauté each ingredient separately till fragrant. Cool and grind together to a fine paste.
- For the mutton curry, heat the oil in a pan; add the sliced onions, cardamoms, cloves and bay leaves; sauté till the onions turn brown. Add the turmeric and chilli powders, hirwa watan, ground spice paste and mutton. Cook, stirring, till the mutton is coated with the spices.
- Add 2 cups water and cook, covered, till the mutton is tender and the gravy thick. Add the goda masala and garam masala and stir to mix. Cook for a few minutes longer and serve hot with rice.

Serves 8

KOMBDICHI SHAGOTI

CHICKEN CURRY WITH ROASTED SPICES AND COCONUT

While Goan chicken xacuti has attained iconic status, many may not know that it is a version of traditional Saraswat Goan shagoti, roasted coconut and spices and all, which was originally made without a souring agent. Though many xacuti recipes are cooked with tamarind, and some even with vinegar, true shagoti is made without either. Here, a little yoghurt has been added to the curry, to lend a slight tang that balances the flavours well.

Ingredients

1kg chicken, cut into 10-12 pieces
½ cup thick coconut milk
1½ tablespoons Hirwa Watan (page 38)
1½ tablespoons oil
10 curry leaves
4 bay leaves
4-5 onions, finely chopped
1½ tablespoons Malwani Masala (page 156)
2 tablespoons Konkani Garam Masala (page 113)
Salt

ONION-COCONUT PASTE
4 onions, sliced
¼ cup fresh coconut, grated
¼ cup dried coconut, grated

Method

- Marinate the chicken in a mixture of the coconut milk and hirwa watan for 30 minutes.
- For the onion-coconut paste, dry-roast the onion, the dried and fresh coconut till fragrant. Cool and grind to a paste.
- Heat the oil in a pan; add the curry leaves, bay leaves and chopped onions. Sauté till the onions turn brown.
- Add the marinated chicken, Malwani masala, onion-coconut paste, Konkani garam masala and salt. Add 2 cups water and cook till the chicken is tender and gravy thick.
- Serve hot with wholewheat phulkas or ghavan (rice flour pancakes).

Serves 8

SARASWAT BANGDA CURRY

SPICY MACKEREL CURRY

I love spicy food. My family and friends will readily vouch for that. And this curry containing red and green chillies is one of the few curries, which immediately satisfy my cravings for something hot and spicy, which surface every now and then. Paired with steamed rice, it is my idea of warm comfort food.

Ingredients

4 tablespoons oil
4 onions, finely chopped
2 teaspoons turmeric powder
1½ teaspoons green chilli paste
10-12 dried red chillies, soaked and ground to a paste
1 whole garlic bulb, cloves separated, and ground to a paste
Salt
½ cup tamarind pulp
1kg mackerel, cut into 2 or 3 pieces each
Coriander leaves, chopped

SPICE PASTE
1 fresh coconut, grated and dry-roasted
1½ teaspoons cumin seeds
30 black peppercorns
2½ teaspoons coriander seeds

Method

- Grind all the ingredients for the spice paste.
- Heat the oil in a pan; add the chopped onions and sauté till golden brown. Add the turmeric, green chilli paste, red chilli paste and garlic paste; sauté till the oil separates.
- Add the spice paste, salt, tamarind pulp and 2 cups water to make a moderately thick curry. When the curry comes to a boil, add the fish pieces, and cook for 5 minutes.
- Garnish with coriander leaves and serve hot with steamed rice.

Serves 6

KONKANI KOMBDI SUKKE

Dry Chicken with Coconut and Spices

If ever this dish was put up in a competition for USP, it would definitely win because of the rare aspect of the spice blend used. The blend is made by grinding spices with fresh coconut, despite which, it can be stored for about a fortnight without any refrigeration! The secret lies in the slow and careful dry-roasting of the mixture, that completely removes all the moisture and also solves the potential problem of the dish going rancid because of the high oil content of the coconut.

Ingredients

1kg chicken, cut into 10-12 pieces
1½ teaspoons turmeric powder
Salt
1 fresh coconut, grated
1½ tablespoons Konkani Garam Masala (page 113)
3 tablespoons oil
3 onions, finely chopped
1 tablespoon ginger-garlic paste
3 tomatoes, finely chopped
2½ tablespoons tamarind pulp

Method

- Marinate the chicken in a mixture of turmeric powder and salt.
- In a frying pan, dry-roast the grated coconut till brown. Remove and grind with the Konkani garam masala.
- Heat the oil in a wok; add the chopped onion and sauté till brown. Add the ginger-garlic paste and sauté for a few seconds.
- Add the chopped tomatoes, coconut spice paste and chicken and sauté till the oil separates.
- Add the salt and tamarind pulp and cook till chicken is tender and the gravy is dry.
- Serve hot with rotis and salad.

Serves 6

SHAHLYATLE MAASE

SEAFOOD AND TENDER COCONUT CURRY

Tender green coconut is 'shahala' in Marathi; one of the staple drinks in Konkan is 'shahalyache paani' or tender coconut water. It is not often one hears of tender coconut water used in cooking. Both the water and the flesh of green coconuts lend a delicate sweetness to this creamy seafood curry enriched with cashew nuts.

Ingredients

3-4 tablespoons oil
2-3 bay leaves
1 cup Browned Onion Paste (page 103)
1½ teaspoons ginger-garlic paste
1 teaspoon turmeric powder
1½ tablespoons Garam Masala (page 34)
1 tablespoon fresh coriander paste
3 cups tender coconut meat, puréed
½ cup cashew nut paste
2 tablespoons tamarind pulp
1 potato, peeled and quartered
1 cup tender coconut water
½kg boneless fish, cut into 5-cm cubes
½kg prawns, peeled and deveined
2 cups Coconut Milk (page 54)
Salt

Method

- Heat the oil in a pan; add the bay leaves and onion paste and sauté for a few seconds. Add the ginger-garlic paste, turmeric powder, garam masala, coriander paste, tender coconut purée, cashew nut paste and tamarind pulp. Stir well and cook for a couple of minutes for the flavours to blend.
- Add the potatoes and tender coconut water and cook till the potatoes are almost done.
- Add the fish and prawns along with the coconut milk and salt. Cook for 2-3 minutes till the fish is just tender.
- Serve hot with rotis or rice.

Serves 4

KOMBDI HIRWA MASALA

GREEN CHICKEN CURRY

Judging by its popularity, it would seem that every Konkani has hirwa (green) masala flowing in his or her veins. It is the most simple of all recipes and is quickly mastered even by first time cooks. It is versatile too and can be used to prepare chicken, meat, fish or vegetable dishes. This recipe is from the Ratnagiri district and one that I treasure.

Ingredients

1 fresh coconut, grated
2 cups chopped coriander leaves
12 green chillies, chopped
5-cm piece ginger
1kg chicken, cut into 10-12 pieces
1 tablespoon ginger-garlic paste
Salt
4 tablespoons oil
4 onions, finely chopped
4 cloves
3 (2.5-cm) cinnamon sticks
6 green cardamom pods
4 black cardamom pods
1½ teaspoons cumin seeds
2 bay leaves
1 teaspoon turmeric powder
1 cup Coconut Milk (page 54)
2 tablespoons Garam Masala (page 34)

Method

- Grind the coconut, chopped coriander, green chillies and ginger to a fine paste.
- Marinate the chicken in a mixture of the ginger-garlic paste and salt.
- Heat the oil in a pan; add the chopped onion and the cloves, cinnamon, green and black cardamoms, cumin seeds and bay leaves. Sauté till the onions turn pink.
- Add the turmeric powder, ground paste and chicken. Sauté till the chicken is lightly browned. Stir in the coconut milk and garam masala; cook till chicken is tender.
- Serve hot with rice or a light pulao.

Serves 8

PAPLETCHI AMTI

POMFRET CURRY WITH TIRPHAL

The term 'amti' usually denotes a thin lentil broth. Here, it describes the thin consistency of the silky, smooth curry in which the fish is cooked. Flavoured predominantly with tirphal, a relative of the Sichuan pepper, and black Tellicherry peppercorns, this fragrant, peppery and tangy curry is a particular favourite of my son Saahil, who, if he had his way, would eat it for dinner every single day.

Ingredients

1kg pomfret, sliced across the bone
Salt
1 teaspoon turmeric powder
Juice of 1 lime
15-20 dried red Kashmiri chillies
2½ tablespoons coriander seeds
1 large fresh coconut, grated
1 teaspoon tirphal/teppal
1½ teaspoons black peppercorns
1 whole garlic bulb, cloves separated and peeled
4 tablespoons oil
4 onions, finely chopped
1 cup tamarind pulp
Coriander leaves, chopped

Method

- Marinate the fish slices in a mixture of salt, turmeric and lime juice for 20 minutes.
- Soak the dried red chillies and coriander seeds in hot water for 15 minutes.
- Grind the grated coconut, red chillies, coriander seeds, tirphal, black peppercorns and garlic to a fine paste.
- Heat the oil in a pan; add the chopped onions and sauté till brown. Add the ground paste and sauté till the oil separates. Add the tamarind pulp, salt and 1½ cups water and bring to a boil. Cook for 5-10 minutes.
- Remove from heat and pass the curry through a strainer. Return the strained curry to the pan and bring to a boil. Add the fish slices and cook for 2 minutes. Garnish with coriander leaves.
- Serve hot with rice.

Serves 4

SANGAMESHWARI KOMBDI

CHICKEN WITH FRESH AND ROASTED CASHEW NUTS

My grand-aunt was very particular when it came to making certain traditional dishes and this was one of them. Firstly, she insisted on fresh cashew nuts sourced from Sangameshwar in Ratnagiri district which is famous for its high quality nuts. She also considered it blasphemous to use any modern equipment such as an electric mixer or grinder - the spice paste had to be ground on a stone. And having tasted her cooking, I must say, grinding spices on a stone makes a world of a difference to the texture and flavour of the dish that no electric gadget can match.

Ingredients

1kg chicken, cut into 10-12 pieces
1 tablespoon ginger-garlic paste
1 teaspoon turmeric powder
Salt
1 cup grated dried coconut, roasted
½ cup dried cashew nuts, roasted, plus to garnish
4 tablespoons oil
6 onions, finely chopped
½ cup Red Chilli Paste (page 29)
2 tablespoons red chilli powder
1½ tablespoons Konkani Garam Masala (page 113)
1½ cups fresh tender cashew nuts, peeled and boiled in water till half cooked

Method

- Marinate the chicken in a mixture of ginger-garlic paste, turmeric and salt for 20 minutes.
- Grind the dried coconut and roasted cashew nuts to a fine paste.
- Heat the oil in a pan; add the chopped onions and sauté till brown. Add the coconut-cashew paste, chilli paste, chilli powder and garam masala; sauté till the oil separates.
- Add the chicken and 1 cup water and cook till almost done. Add the tender cashew nuts and cook till the chicken is tender and the curry thickens.
- Serve with rice bhakri or ghavan.

Serves 4 to 6

BANGDA UDID METHI

MACKEREL CURRY WITH BLACK GRAM AND FENUGREEK SEEDS

This is one of the first recipes I ever collected – the beginning of a lifelong journey. I was in the tenth standard when I first tasted this curry at lunch at a friend's home and instantly fell in love with it. I pleaded with his mother to teach me how to cook it. Though amused, she relented and I studiously took copious notes, which are with me to this day.

Ingredients

SPICE PASTE
4 tablespoons oil
½ cup grated fresh coconut
1½ tablespoons coriander seeds
1½ tablespoons raw rice
10 dried red chillies
1 tablespoon split black gram
1½ teaspoons fenugreek seeds
¼ teaspoon asafoetida
8-10 curry leaves
3 onions, finely chopped
1½ tablespoons ginger-garlic paste
1½ tablespoons red chilli powder
1½ tablespoons black peppercorns
½ cup tamarind pulp
Salt
1kg mackerels, each cut into 2 or 3 pieces

Method

- Heat 1 tablespoon oil in a frying pan; add the grated coconut, coriander seeds, raw rice and red chillies; sauté till the coconut turns brown. Cool and grind with a little water to a fine paste.
- Heat the remaining oil in a wok; add the split black gram, fenugreek seeds and asafoetida and sauté for a few seconds. Add the curry leaves, onions and ginger-garlic paste, and sauté until the onions turn light brown.
- Add the ground paste, chilli powder, peppercorns, tamarind pulp, salt and 1 cup water. Stir to mix and cook for a few minutes.
- Add the mackerels and cook for a few minutes till the fish is just cooked.
- Serve hot with rice bhakris or wholewheat phulkas.

Serves 6

TEESRYACHE SUKKE

CLAMS WITH COCONUT AND SPICES

Selecting clams can be a tricky business. Choose only those that are heavy and tightly shut. Discard any that are opened even a crack. Clams, mussels and oysters are pearls of the ocean and great favourites with coastal communities. There are so many different ways of cooking clams, but almost all of them involve the use of coconut, usually coarsely ground, to provide a textural contrast to the soft meat.

Ingredients

2 tablespoons oil
3 onions, finely chopped
1½ tablespoons Hirwa Watan (page 38)
½ cup Browned Onion paste (page 103)
½ cup roasted dried coconut paste
½ cup tamarind pulp
2 tablespoons Koli Masala (page 94)
1 tablespoon Garam Masala (page 34)
1 teaspoon turmeric powder
Salt
1kg clams

Method

- Heat the oil in a wok; add the chopped onions and sauté till brown.
- Add the hirwa watan, onion and coconut pastes and the rest of the ingredients, except the clams. Sauté for 2 minutes.
- Add the clams and cook till tender and dry. Discard any clams that do not open.
- Serve hot with phulkas.

Serves 6

MORI KHEEMA

Minced Shark with Garlic and Spices

Usually made for breakfast or a quick snack, this spiced shark mince, tastes especially good when mixed with some dry garlic chutney and rolled up in a bajra (millet) roti. I always make this for my best friend Marzaban, who prefers to eat it with hot buttered toast.

Ingredients

2 tablespoons Hirwa Watan (page 38)
Juice of 1 lime
1½ tablespoons Garam Masala (page 34)
1 tablespoon turmeric powder
Salt
1kg shark, boiled, skinned, deboned and shredded or minced
3 tablespoons oil
2 small garlic bulbs, cloves peeled and chopped
Coriander leaves, to garnish

Method

- In a bowl, combine all the ingredients, except the oil, garlic and coriander.
- Heat the oil in a pan; add the chopped garlic and sauté for 2 minutes.
- Add the mixed ingredients and cook on high heat for 2 minutes.
- Serve hot, garnished with chopped coriander leaves.

Serves 6

BANGDYACHE SUKKE

QUICK SPICY MACKEREL

This is a recipe I like to make when out on a picnic as it is quick and easy to prepare. All it requires is a pan, a spoon, some clean water and a small fire. I carry the mackerel in an icebox and all the other ingredients tossed together in a small ziplock bag. I sometimes also grind all the other ingredients together and carry them as a spice paste, which makes things even quicker and more delicious.

Ingredients

4 mackerels
8 green chillies, sliced
1 cup grated fresh coconut, plus to garnish
5 kokum rinds
10 tirphal/teppal
1½ tablespoons ginger-garlic paste
2 tablespoons red chilli powder
1 tablespoon turmeric powder
Salt
Coriander leaves, to garnish

Method

- Place the mackerel and the rest of the ingredients along with a little water in a pan, and cook till the mackerels are tender and the gravy clings to the fish.
- Serve hot, garnished with chopped coriander leaves and grated coconut.

Serves 4

SHINGADYACHE KALWAN

CATFISH CURRY

This is one of the simplest and most common curries you will find in the region. The fish may vary, but the ingredients and method remain the same: coconut, dried red chillies and garlic, with a souring agent, usually tamarind or kokum which grows in abundance in the region. Everything, except the fish goes into the pan, and bubbles away for a few minutes before the fish is thrown in. Eaten with boiled or steamed rice, this is staple coastal fare to be enjoyed with pickle or fried fish on the side.

Ingredients

2½ tablespoons oil
4 onions, finely chopped
1 fresh coconut, grated
7 tablespoons red chilli powder
1 tablespoon turmeric powder
1 bulb garlic, cloves separated and peeled
20 black peppercorns
½ cup tamarind pulp
4 kokum rinds
Salt
4 catfish cut into pieces

Method

- Heat the oil in a wok; add the chopped onions and sauté till light brown and soft.
- Add the rest of the ingredients, except the fish, and enough water to make a thick curry. Bring to a boil and cook for about 5 minutes.
- Add the fish and cook for 3 minutes.
- Serve hot with steamed rice.

Serves 6

KOLAMBI BATATA TONDAK

Prawns and Potatoes in a Thick Coconut Curry

The term, 'tondak,' usually denotes a dish of vegetables or legumes cooked in a thick coconut gravy. This recipe is from Ratnagiri. The potatoes grown in this region have a unique flavour and starch content owing to the red soil in which they are cultivated. Often cooked together with mutton, here the potatoes find a worthy companion in jumbo prawns.

Ingredients

1½ tablespoons oil
1 teaspoon turmeric powder
6 tablespoons tamarind pulp
10 baby potatoes, peeled
Salt
1kg jumbo prawns, peeled and deveined with tails intact

Spice paste
1 fresh coconut, grated
3 onions, sliced
2 garlic bulbs, cloves separated and peeled
20 dried red chillies
1½ tablespoons poppy seeds
1½ tablespoons fennel seeds
4 (2.5-cm) cinnamon sticks
4 star anise
20 black peppercorns
10 tirphal/teppal
1½ tablespoons coriander seeds

Method

- For the spice paste, dry roast all the ingredients till fragrant but not brown. Cool and grind to a fine paste.
- Heat the oil in a pan; add the spice paste, turmeric powder, tamarind pulp, potatoes, salt and 1 cup water. Cook till the potatoes are soft.
- Add the prawns and cook for 3 minutes.
- Serve hot with rotis.

Serves 6

KOLAMBI BIRYANI

BIRYANI WITH PRAWNS COOKED IN COCONUT MILK

This biryani can be made with either saltwater or fresh water prawns. I personally prefer the fresh water variety as they have a certain sweetness which gives the biryani an unparalleled flavour.

Ingredients

PRAWNS

1 cup thick Coconut Milk (page 54)
1½ teaspoons clove powder
1½ teaspoons cinnamon powder
1½ teaspoons green cardamom powder
1 teaspoon turmeric powder
Salt
1kg prawns, shelled and deveined
8 tablespoons ghee
2 large onions, finely chopped
5 green chillies, slit
2 teaspoons red chilli powder
2 teaspoons Konkani Garam Masala (page 113)
2 tomatoes, puréed
1 tablespoon ginger-garlic paste

RICE

8 tablespoons ghee
8 green cardamom pods
5 bay leaves
3 large onions, sliced
1 tablespoon ginger-garlic paste
3 tomatoes, boiled and puréed
1 teaspoon chilli powder (optional)
1½ teaspoons coriander powder
1 cup chopped coriander leaves (optional)
1 cup boiled green peas (optional)
Salt
Juice of 1 lime
3 cups long-grained rice
A big pinch of saffron, soaked in warm milk
5 green chillies, slit

Method

- For the prawns, combine the coconut milk, ¾ teaspoon clove powder, ¾ teaspoon cinnamon powder, ¾ teaspoon cardamom powder, turmeric and salt. Add the prawns, mix well and leave to marinate in a refrigerator for 6 hours.
- Heat the ghee in a pan; add the chopped onions and sauté till brown. Add the green chillies, chilli powder and garam masala; sauté for a minute.
- Add the marinated prawns, tomato purée and ginger-garlic paste and sauté for 5 minutes. Add a little salt and cook till almost dry.
- For the rice, heat the ghee in a pan; add the cardamoms, bay leaves and the onions. Sauté till the onions turn light brown. Add the ginger-garlic paste and sauté for a few seconds. Add the tomato purée, chilli powder and coriander powder and sauté for 2 minutes.
- Add 10 cups of water, the coriander leaves, green peas, salt and lime juice. When the water starts boiling, add the rice and cook till half done.
- Drain the water from the rice and mix in the saffron soaked in milk.
- To assemble the biryani, spread the prawn mixture in a heavy-bottomed pan; top with the rice and seal the pan with a tight-fitting lid. Cook on a low heat for about 20 minutes till the rice is tender.
- Serve hot with a raita of your choice and roasted papad.

Serves 8

PAPLET HIRWA MASALA

POMFRET IN GREEN COCONUT CURRY

My Parsi friends refer to this dish as the Maharashtrian version of patra ni macchi, though this thick curry is not at all like the Parsi fish steamed in banana leaves, except for the green coriander chutney both dishes share. I love dishes like these, which echo flavours in other cuisines. In my opinion, they help transcend cultural differences by showing that food and flavour, at least, have no boundaries.

Ingredients

2 medium pomfrets
Salt
1½ teaspoons cumin seeds
10 black peppercorns
6 cloves
3 (2.5-cm) cinnamon sticks
5 green chillies
2 cups coriander leaves, chopped
1 tablespoon oil
½ cup finely chopped onion
1½ teaspoons ginger-garlic paste
1½ teaspoons turmeric powder
1½ teaspoons coriander powder
1 cup grated fresh coconut
½ cup chopped coriander leaves

Method

- Cut the fish into 2.5-cm thick slices. Sprinkle with salt and set aside.
- Grind the cumin seeds, peppercorns, cloves, cinnamon, green chillies and coriander leaves to a fine paste.
- Heat the oil in a pan; add the chopped onion and sauté for 2-3 minutes till they soften. Add the ground spice paste, ginger-garlic paste, turmeric and coriander powders and grated coconut; fry till the oil separates.
- Add 1½ cups water and cook till the gravy thickens. Gently slide the sliced pomfret into the gravy and cook for 5 minutes.
- Serve hot with steamed rice.

Serves 4

MORI LAL MASALA

Shark in a Spicy Red Curry

I first tasted this dish at a friend's home in Girgaum in central Mumbai. One of the main ingredients in this recipe is kokum (the dried rind of a fruit of the mangosteen family), that not only gives the dish a delicious tang, but also a beautiful colour. Today, with kokum agal (concentrate) being available in stores across Maharashtra, preparing this dish has become much easier and saves on time as well.

Ingredients

1 small shark, skinned and cut into 5-cm cubes
Salt
1½ tablespoons oil
¼ cup chopped onions
2 cups water
2 teaspoons kokum pulp, or to taste
½ cup chopped coriander leaves, to garnish

Spice paste

½ cup fresh coconut, grated
4 dried red chillies
1½ teaspoons chopped ginger
1½ teaspoons chopped garlic
1½ teaspoons poppy seeds
1½ teaspoons coriander powder
1 teaspoon fennel seeds
¾ teaspoon mace
½ teaspoon grated nutmeg
4 cloves
6 black peppercorns
1 black cardamom pod
1 small bay leaf

Method

- Rub salt all over the shark pieces. Wash and drain. Repeat the process and pat the pieces dry.
- For the spice paste, dry-roast the ingredients in a frying pan or griddle till fragrant. Cool and grind with a little water to a fine paste.
- Heat the oil in a pan; add the chopped onions and sauté till brown. Add the spice paste and sauté, sprinkling a little water, to prevent the paste from burning.
- Add the kokum pulp, salt and the fish; sauté for a minute to coat the fish with the spices. Add 1 cup water and cook till the fish is tender.
- Garnish with coriander leaves and serve hot with steamed rice.

Serves 4

BHARLELA PAPLET

FRIED POMFRET STUFFED WITH CORIANDER CHUTNEY

Green coriander chutney is a versatile condiment which can be used as a base for a curry, served on the side with hot bhajis (fritters) or used to stuff vegetables and, in this case, fish. The creamy white flesh of the pomfret is the perfect foil for the spicy chutney, and when fried crisp on the outside, it is irresistible.

Ingredients

500g pomfret (1 large or 2 small)
2 tablespoons tamarind pulp
1 teaspoon turmeric powder
3 teaspoons red chilli powder
2 teaspoons Koli Masala (page 94)
1 teaspoon Garam Masala (page 34)
Salt to taste
6 tablespoons oil

CORIANDER CHUTNEY
1 small cup fresh coriander
4 green chillies
12 garlic cloves
2.5-cm piece ginger

Method

- Grind all the ingredients for the coriander chutney to a fine paste.
- Remove the centre bone of the pomfret by slitting the fish carefully on either side of the bone. Or request your fishmonger to remove the bone. Wash the fish and make horizontal gashes on both sides.
- Combine the tamarind pulp, turmeric and chilli powders, Koli masala, garam masala and salt. Rub the mixture all over the fish. Stuff the fish with the coriander chutney.
- Heat the oil in a large frying pan; place the fish in the pan and fry till brown on both sides, turning it carefully.
- Serve with phulkas.

Serves 2

KOMBDICHA MOTLA

Chicken in Turmeric Leaf Parcels

This is a recipe that I like to serve at large parties because I can prepare the parcels in advance. In the Konkan belt, turmeric leaves are popular wrappers for steamed dishes, including patoli (rice and coconut pancakes) as they provide a delicate fragrance and flavour. Serve the chicken in the leaves and watch the dish create a stir.

Ingredients

1kg boneless chicken, cut into 5-cm pieces
1 teaspoon turmeric powder
2 teaspoons red chilli powder
2½ teaspoons Konkani Garam Masala (page 113)
2 tablespoons tamarind pulp
Salt
1 large banana leaf
2-3 turmeric leaves
Oil as required

Spice paste
2 tablespoons grated dried coconut, dry-roasted
2 onions, sliced and dry-roasted
1 teaspoon tirphal/teppal, roasted
1 teaspoon coriander seeds, roasted
2 teaspoons oil
2 tablespoons grated fresh coconut
3 tablespoons Hirwa Watan (page 38)

Method

- For the spice paste, individually dry-roast the grated dried coconut, sliced onion, tirphal and coriander seeds in a frying pan. Set aside.
- In the same frying pan, heat 1 teaspoon oil and sauté the grated fresh coconut till golden brown; remove and set aside. Heat the remaining 1 teaspoon oil and fry the hirwa watan for a few minutes and remove. Grind the roasted and sautéed spices to a paste.
- Combine the spice paste, turmeric and chilli powders, garam masala, tamarind pulp and salt and marinate the chicken in the mixture for 30 minutes.
- Lay a clean banana leaf on a work surface. Lay the turmeric leaves on the banana leaf. Place the marinated chicken in the centre and fold the leaves over to enclose the chicken and make a package (motla). Secure with kitchen twine.
- Place the leaf package in a kadhai or large pan, cover with a lid and cook on moderate heat for about 20-25 minutes till the chicken is tender.
- Open up the package and serve at once.

Note: if the chicken releases a lot of water, remove the chicken pieces and cook the gravy till dry in a pan.

Serves 6

KONKANI KHEKDA MASALA

CRAB CURRY

I have not yet met a seafood lover who does not drool over a spicy crab curry. The pleasures of picking out the meat with one's fingers and then chewing on the tender shells and claws to extract every ounce of spicy juice are impossible to resist. Keep some bhakri or pav at hand to mop up the thick gravy.

Ingredients

1 teaspoon turmeric powder
2-3 bay leaves
Salt
4 large sea crabs, cleaned and cut into pieces
6 tablespoons oil
7 onions, finely chopped
1½ teaspoons ginger-garlic paste
1 cup fresh tomato purée
½ cup tamarind pulp
1 tablespoon jaggery
Salt
6 green chillies, slit
2 teaspoons mustard seeds
Chopped coriander, to garnish
Fresh grated coconut, to garnish

SPICE PASTE

1 tablespoon oil
1 fresh coconut, grated
10 green cardamom pods
10 cloves
2.5-cm cinnamon stick
2 teaspoons poppy seeds
2 teaspoons coriander seeds
1½ teaspoons cumin seeds
A few pieces of mace
8 dried red Kashmiri chillies, boiled in water for 10 minutes

Method

- Bring 2 large cups of water to a boil in a pan; add ½ teaspoon turmeric powder, the bay leaves, salt and the crab. Cook for 10 minutes. Remove from the heat and set aside.
- For the spice paste, heat the oil in a frying pan or griddle. Add the coconut, and sauté till brown. Remove and set aside.
- In the same frying pan, dry-roast the rest of the ingredients, except the boiled red chillies. Cool and grind with the browned coconut and boiled chillies to a fine paste.
- For the curry, heat 5 tablespoons oil in a pan; sauté the onions till golden brown. Add the ginger-garlic paste and remaining turmeric powder dissolved in a little water; sauté for 2 minutes.
- Add the spice paste, tomato purée, tamarind pulp, jaggery and salt; sauté till the oil separates. Add the slit green chillies and the crab along with the stock and cook till the gravy thickens.
- In a small kadhai, heat the remaining oil; add the mustard seeds and when they splutter pour them over the crab curry.
- Garnish with coriander leaves and grated coconut and serve with bhakri or pav.

Serves 4

Malwan

MALWANI MASALA

MALWANI MUTTON SUKKE

MALWANI KOMBDI MASALA

MALWANI KHEKDA SUKKE

KARLI MASALA

MORICHE SUKKE

A Konkani fish curry by any other name should taste the same – but not if it is Malwani. Although the town of Malwan and surrounding region in the Sindhudurg district lie along the Konkan coastline, it has carved out a distinct cuisine of its own that has recently come into the limelight.

Malwani food is based on the four pillars of Konkani food: seafood, rice, coconut and kokum, all of which abound in the region. But it is the spice mix – the Malwani masala which gives it a unique identity. The combination and proportion of spices, including the large quantity of tirphal or teppal, the tongue-numbing spice which is related to the Sichuan peppercorn, produce fiery curries which are redder and hotter than most other Konkani curries, and in direct contrast to the cool, pristine waters of its own picturesque beach and the ones close by like Tarkarli.

Fresh crabs, lobster, prawns and fish of all sizes and shapes find themselves in bubbling coconut curries or fried in oil over wood fires. Kokum, the dried rind of the fruit belonging to the mangosteen family, is the souring agent most Malwanis prefer as groves of the garcinia Indica tree cover the hillsides. They provide a mellow tang to the curries and also form the base for one of the region's most famous drinks – solkadi. This refreshing, beverage made of kokum concentrate and coconut milk, spiked with garlic, ginger, green chillies and coriander leaves, provides a soothing accompaniment to douse the flames of a fiery curry.

Mutton and chicken dishes served with jowari bhakri (sorghum flatbreads) are cooked on special occasions, like the famous Dashavtar, which is a theatrical representation of the ten avatars of Lord Vishnu, where all the roles are played by women. It is a time for fun and feasting and Malwan pulls out all the culinary stops: in addition to the array of dishes, Malwanis showcase their famous khaja and ladoos. At celebrations like these, and indeed in everyday meals, vegetables always take second place.

Not far from the town of Malwan, the landmark Sindhudurg fort which towers over the surrounding area could very well symbolise the place Malwani cuisine has earned for itself – prominent, strong, hearty and a force to reckon with.

MALWANI MASALA

MALWAN SPICE MIX

The bold flavours of the cuisine of this tiny town are reflected in its basic spice blend. A whole year's supply is prepared in the hot summer months or just after the monsoon. It adds flavour and depth to seafood dishes, meats, vegetables and lentils. While one may think the dishes all wind up tasting the same, the magic of the spice blend lies in bringing out the intrinsic flavour of the core ingredient and embellishing it with flavours that are complementary, yet distinct.

Ingredients

250g dried red chillies
1½ teaspoons mustard seeds
1 tablespoon tirphal/teppal
1 tablespoon poppy seeds
1 tablespoon black cumin seeds
1½ teaspoons fenugreek seeds
1½ teaspoons cloves
8 (2.5-cm) cinnamon sticks
2 nutmegs, grated
1 tablespoon fennel seeds
1½ tablespoons coriander seeds
15 black cardamom pods
2-3 star anise
1½ teaspoons black peppercorns
3 pieces dried turmeric root
1½ teaspoons mace

Method

- Dry-roast the spices in a frying pan or griddle till fragrant.
- Cool and grind to a fine powder.
- Store in an airtight jar

Makes about 1 cup

MALWANI MUTTON SUKKE

STIR-FRIED MUTTON WITH COCONUT AND SPICES

Malwani cuisine revolves around seafood. However, on special occasions, mutton or chicken take centre stage. This dry mutton dish stir-fried with fragrant spices and coconut is a particular favourite, especially if eaten with chapatti or bhakri, with onion rings, whole green chillies and a couple of lemon wedges on the side.

Ingredients

1kg mutton on the bone, cut into 5-cm pieces
1 tablespoon turmeric powder
Salt
3 tablespoons oil
4 onions, finely chopped
1 tablespoon ginger-garlic paste
2 tablespoons red chilli powder
1 fresh coconut, grated
1 tablespoon Malwani Masala (page 156)
1½ teaspoons Garam Masala (page 34)
2 tablespoons thick tamarind pulp
½ cup fried cashew nuts, to garnish

Method

- In a pan, combine the mutton, turmeric, salt and 2-3 cups of water. Bring to a boil, lower the heat and simmer till the mutton is tender. Drain and reserve the mutton.
- Heat the oil in a wok; add the chopped onion and sauté till brown. Add the ginger-garlic paste, chilli powder, grated coconut, Malwani masala and garam masala; sauté till fragrant.
- Add the cooked meat, salt and tamarind pulp and cook on high heat, stirring continuously, till dry and well coated with the spices.
- Serve hot, garnished with fried cashew nuts.

Serves 4 to 6

MALWANI KOMBDI MASALA

Clay pot Chicken Curry

The only way to cook this dish, in my opinion, is in an earthenware or clay pot. The flavour of the clay seeps into the curry giving it an earthy flavour that a steel or non-stick pan just cannot. In addition, the fresh herby flavour of green masala, rich sweetness of roasted coconut and robust zing of Malwani masala come together to make this an unforgettable dish.

Ingredients

Spice paste

6 tablespoons oil

Flesh of 1 fresh coconut, sliced

5 onions, sliced

20 garlic cloves

5-cm piece ginger, chopped

6 green chillies

1 cup fresh coriander, chopped

Chicken curry

1-2 tablespoons oil

1 teaspoon turmeric powder

2 teaspoons red chilli powder

1½ tablespoons Malwani Masala (page 156)

1½ teaspoons Garam Masala (page 34)

1kg chicken, cut into 10-12 pieces

Juice of one lime

1 cup coconut milk

Salt

Method

- For the spice paste, heat 2 tablespoons oil in a frying pan or griddle and roast the coconut slices till brown. Remove and reserve.
- Add 2 more tablespoons oil to the frying pan; add the sliced onion and sauté till brown and set aside.
- Add the remaining oil; sauté the garlic, ginger, chillies and coriander for a minute. Grind all the fried ingredients to a fine paste.
- For the chicken curry, heat the oil in a pan, or preferably, an earthenware cooking pot. Add the spice paste, turmeric powder, chilli powder, Malwani masala and garam masala and stir to mix. Add the chicken and sauté for 2 minutes.
- Add 2 cups warm water and the lime juice and cook till the chicken is tender.
- Stir in the coconut milk and salt, and cook on a low heat for about 5 minutes, or till the gravy is moderately thick.
- Serve hot with sorghum bhakris and onion wedges.

Serves 8

MALWANI KHEKDA SUKKE

SPICED CRABS WITH GARLIC AND COCONUT

The number of dishes one discovers in the tiniest, most unassuming, places is quite amazing. This is one such example. My first introduction to this mouth-watering crab dish came about when I was travelling through a small town called Kudal in the Sindhudurg district of Maharashtra. I was driving past a khanaval (roadside eatery) when I caught a whiff of an irresistible aroma, which made me so hungry I decided to follow it to the source. Imagine my excitement when the owner not only fed me this dish, but also shared his precious recipe with me!

Ingredients

4 large mud crabs
4 tablespoons oil
3 onions, sliced
2 cups grated fresh coconut
5-cm piece ginger, chopped
2 garlic bulbs, cloves separated, peeled and chopped
½ tablespoon mustard seeds
2 sprigs curry leaves
1 tablespoon Malwani Masala (page 156)
1½ tablespoons red chilli powder
½ tablespoon turmeric powder
Salt
6 tablespoons tamarind pulp

Method

- Clean the crabs and cut each one in half.
- Heat 2 tablespoons oil in a pan; add the onions, coconut, ginger and garlic and sauté till the coconut turns brown. Cool and grind to a fine paste.
- Heat the remaining oil in a wok; add the mustard and curry leaves. When the mustard begins to splutter, add the spice paste and a little water and cook till the oil separates.
- Add the Malwani masala, chilli powder, turmeric powder, salt and the crabs. Stir well, add the tamarind pulp and cook till the crabs are done and the gravy dry.
- Serve with rice bhakris.

Serves 4

KARLI MASALA

Silver Bar-Fish Curry

Karli or silver bar-fish is one of the most delicious fish in the world, but also the most frustrating to eat. This fish has the most number of tiny bones you are likely to encounter in any seafood. Eating the fish proves to be a test of concentration and patience as one has to focus on avoiding the bones and the prospect of one of them lodging itself in the throat. The secret to successfully tackling this difficult fish is in the slicing – best left to the expertise of fishmongers who slice the fish on the diagonal avoiding cutting through the bones, then turn it over and slice it once again on the diagonal.

Ingredients

3 tablespoons oil
2 cups finely chopped onion
1 tablespoon Malwani Masala (page 156)
2 teaspoons turmeric powder
1½ tablespoons tamarind pulp
Salt
1kg silver bar-fish, sliced diagonally

Spice paste
2 tablespoons oil
1 tablespoon raw rice
1 tablespoon split black gram
1½ teaspoons fenugreek seeds
½ fresh coconut, grated
1 teaspoon black peppercorns
1 garlic bulb, cloves separated and peeled
20 dried red Kashmiri chillies
1 cup fried fenugreek leaves

Method

- For the spice paste, heat the oil in a frying pan or griddle; sauté the rice, split black gram, fenugreek seeds, coconut, peppercorns, garlic and chillies. Cool and grind to a fine paste with the fried fenugreek leaves.
- Heat the oil in a pan; add the chopped onions and sauté till brown. Add the spice paste, Malwani masala, turmeric powder, tamarind pulp, salt and 1½ cups water. Bring to a boil, lower the heat and cook till the gravy is thick.
- Add the fish slices and cook for 2 or 3 minutes.
- Serve hot with phulkas.

Serves 6

MORICHE SUKKE

SPICY DRY SHARK CURRY

I first encountered this dish at a dhaba or highway food stall on the road to Goa. The owner had piled up pieces of boiled shark along the edge of a large hot griddle. As an order came in, he would quickly toss a portion of shark meat with a whole lot of spices and serve it up sizzling hot. It's the best thing one can eat on a hot day, especially when washed down with a chilled bottle of beer.

Ingredients

½ cup fresh coconut, grated
½ cup dried coconut, grated
3 onions, finely chopped
3 tablespoons oil
2 onions, sliced
1 tablespoon ginger-garlic paste
1 tablespoon Malwani Masala (page 156)
1½ teaspoons turmeric powder
1½ tablespoons red chilli powder
6 kokum rinds
Salt
1kg shark, skin removed and cut into 5-cm pieces

Method

- Dry-roast the fresh coconut, dried coconut and onions in a frying pan or griddle; cool and grind to a fine paste.
- Heat the oil in a pan; add the chopped onion and sauté till brown. Add the ginger-garlic paste, Malwani masala, turmeric and chilli powders, kokum, the ground paste and salt; sauté till the oil separates.
- Add the fish and 5 tablespoons water. Cover the pan and cook till the fish is tender and well coated with the spices.
- Serve hot with bajra bhakri (pearl millet flatbread) or bread.

Serves 6

Nagpur Saoji & Varhadi

SAOJI MUTTON RASSA

SAOJI KOMBDI

SAOJI MUTTON

SAOJI MACHHI MASALA

NAGPURI DAHI MUTTON

VARHADI MUTTON

VARHADI KOMBDI

NAGPURI METHI KOMBDI

NAGPURI KALA PULAO

NAGPURI KOMBDI MASALA

SAOJI MACHHI FRY

First impressions are lasting impressions that remain with you for life. The first time I ate Saoji mutton rassa is an occasion I will never forget. Having grown up on tear-jerkingly spicy Kolhapuri cuisine, I had approached my first Saoji meal with bravado. Nothing had prepared me for the mind-numbing spice that shocked my whole system and set off a never-ending bout of hiccoughs. I was humbled, but not enough to never try it again: it has now become one of my favourite cuisines.

Saoji is the original food of the Halba Koshti tribe of Madhya Pradesh, who moved to Nagpur and took up weaving as a profession. Their unapologetically tongue-searing dishes have developed a cult following, with ardent fans downing a couple of bowls of gut-scorching rassa (thin gravy) at the start of a meal. What gives the curries their heat are fiery dried red Bhiwapuri chillies combined with other aromatic spices, which produce their own slow burn.

While Saoji cuisine is native to Nagpur, Varhadi cuisine is one of the foods of the Vidarbha region in western Maharashtra of which Nagpur is the capital. Both cuisines are hot and spicy and one is often clubbed with the other to make what is now popularly called Saoji-Varhadi cuisine.

Saoji-Varhadi foods are traditionally cooked in groundnut and linseed or flaxseed oils which are available in abundance in the area. Other regional ingredients like groundnuts, gram flour, jowar (sorghum), poppy seeds and dried coconut add nutrition and texture to the gravies. Jowar is one of the most popular grains used to make bhakri (flatbreads) and dhapoda or jowar papads, which are a speciality of the region. Edmi or spiced wholewheat breads and special lambi roti that are cooked over upturned earthenware pots over a wood fire, are used to mop up the curries, most of which are non-vegetarian.

The range of meat and chicken curries is impressive, including the rhyming shakanu chaknu goat and chicken curry, and black quail curry. And who has not heard of Saoji mutton and Saoji chicken? River fish is available from the rivers around Nagpur, though sadly, the river Nag which flows through the city and for which Nagpur was named by Bulund Shah, the Gond king of Devgad, is too polluted to sustain aquatic life.

That being said, as the home of the sweetest oranges and the spiciest curries in India, Nagpur has a culinary profile of which it can justifiably be proud. A pride which has prompted Saoji food fans to claim for Nagpur's unique Saoji food the much sought after GI (Geographical Indication) status which has already been conferred on Nagpur oranges.

SAOJI MUTTON RASSA

SPICY MUTTON CURRY WITH YOGHURT AND FENUGREEK

Not to be confused with Saoji mutton, this spicy mutton curry has yoghurt and a good deal of dried fenugreek, with some fresh hirwa watan and a dash of coconut oil added to round off the flavours. My grandfather would source the dried fenugreek all the way from Kasur in Pakistan, which is believed to produce the best quality fenugreek in terms of flavour and fragrance. Nagpuris eat this curry with lambi rotis - thin flatbreads cooked on the round bottoms of earthenware pots upturned over hot coals. But any other Indian bread will do.

Ingredients

1kg mutton on the bone, cut into 5-cm pieces
250g yoghurt, whisked
Salt
4 tablespoons groundnut oil
1 cup Browned Onion Paste (page 103)
1½ tablespoons Hirwa Watan (page 38)
1 teaspoon turmeric powder
2 teaspoons red chilli powder
1½ teaspoons dried fenugreek, powdered
1 tablespoon coconut oil
Chopped fresh coriander, to garnish

SPICE PASTE
15-20 dried red Kashmiri chillies
5 (2.5-cm) cinnamon sticks
10 cloves
5 black cardamom pods
1½ teaspoons dried lichen
2 bay leaves
1½ teaspoons poppy seeds
1½ teaspoons black cumin seeds
1½ tablespoons coriander seeds

Method

- In a bowl, combine the mutton, yoghurt and salt. Leave to marinate for at least 2 hours, preferably in a refrigerator.
- For the spice paste, dry-roast the spices on a griddle till fragrant. Boil the roasted spices in 1 cup water for 10 minutes and set aside to cool. Grind to a fine paste.
- Heat the oil in a pan; add the browned onion paste and hirwa watan and sauté for a minute. Add the rest of the ingredients including the coconut oil and sauté till the oil separates.
- Add the mutton and sauté for a few minutes till the spices coat the meat. Stir in 3 cups water and bring to a boil. Lower the heat and cook, covered, till the mutton is tender and the gravy is thick.
- Garnish with chopped coriander leaves and serve with roti, bhakri or rice.

Serves 6 to 8

SAOJI KOMBDI

SPICY CHICKEN CURRY WITH CASHEW NUTS AND COCONUT

A trip to Nagpur would be incomplete without a taste of the famous Saoji Chicken or Mutton. It would be reasonable to believe that the recipes for both these iconic dishes would be the same, but the truth is they are completely different. The chicken version has, in addition to the usual spices, a hefty amount of the Maharashtrian staple goda masala, and split Bengal gram, rice grains and cashew nuts to add body and thickness to the curry. Jowar (sorghum) flour is sometimes used to thicken the curry as well.

Ingredients

SPICE PASTE

10-12 dried red Kashmiri chillies
2 tablespoons groundnut oil
1 tablespoon poppy seeds
1½ tablespoons sesame seeds
1 tablespoon dried lichen
1½ teaspoons black cumin seeds
1 tablespoon coriander seeds
2½ tablespoons grated dried coconut
2 tablespoons cashew nuts
1 tablespoon split Bengal gram
1½ teaspoons raw rice

FOR THE CHICKEN CURRY

2 tablespoons groundnut oil
3 Roasted Onions (page 42), ground to a paste
1½ tablespoons ginger-garlic paste
1 teaspoon green chilli paste
1 teaspoon cumin powder
½ teaspoon turmeric powder
2 teaspoons red chilli powder
1½ tablespoons Garam Masala (page 34)
2 tablespoons Goda Masala (page 33)
1kg chicken, cut into 8-10 pieces

Method

- For the spice paste, heat the oil in a frying pan and sauté all the ingredients till fragrant. Cool and grind into a fine paste.
- For the chicken curry, heat the oil in a pan; add the roasted onion paste, ginger-garlic paste, green chilli paste and cumin powder; sauté till the oil separates.
- Add the turmeric, chilli powder, garam masala and goda masala, and sauté on medium heat till the oil separates.
- Add the chicken and salt and stir to coat with the spices. Add 2 cups water and bring to a boil. Lower the heat and cook, partially covered, till the chicken is tender and the gravy thickens.
- Serve hot with jowar bhakri, roti, or rice.

Serves 4 to 6

SAOJI MUTTON

Spicy Mutton Curry

The list of spices seems endless but every one of them plays a role in earning for this dish both accolades and tears. You can tone down the spice levels if you like, but for a genuine Saoji experience the tears must flow and the tongue must be on fire. Keep a bowl of soothing yoghurt handy to put out the flames – sips of chilled beer might also help.

Ingredients

Spice paste

½ cup groundnut oil
8 onions, thinly sliced
15 dried red Kashmiri chillies
1 cup grated dried coconut
1 tablespoon coriander seeds
1 tablespoon black cumin seeds
10 cloves
20 black peppercorns
6 green cardamom pods
6 black cardamoms pods
5 (2.5-cm) cinnamon sticks
5 bay leaves
1½ teaspoons poppy seeds
1½ tablespoons dried lichen

Mutton curry

1½ tablespoons ginger-garlic paste
2kg mutton on the bone, cut into 5-cm pieces
Salt
Chopped coriander leaves, to garnish

Method

- For the spice paste, heat the oil in a pan; fry the sliced onions for 2 minutes.
- Drain and grind the fried onions with the rest of the spices to a fine paste. Strain the oil.
- In another pan, heat the strained oil; add the ginger-garlic paste, and sauté for a minute.
- Add the spice paste, mutton and salt and mix well till the mutton is coated well with the spices. Stir in 3-4 cups water and bring to a boil. Lower the heat and simmer, partially covered, till the mutton is tender and gravy is thick.
- Sprinkle with chopped coriander and serve with rice, roti or bhakri.

Serves 10 to 12

SAOJI MACHHI MASALA

FRIED FISH IN THICK SPICY GRAVY

Rohu (Indian carp) or any freshwater fish is ideal for this dish from landlocked Nagpur. The fleshy slices are fried lightly before adding them to the gravy, which gives the fish a firmer texture. As is expected of Saoji food, the spices are aplenty and the flavours bold, but tempered somewhat with grated coconut, melon seeds and cashew nuts.

Ingredients

1kg Indian carp, cleaned and sliced across the bone
Salt
1½ teaspoons turmeric powder
Juice of 2 limes
4 tablespoons oil
1½ tablespoons Browned Onion Paste (page 103)
1½ teaspoons Goda Masala (page 33)

SPICE PASTE
1 tablespoon groundnut oil
1 cup grated dried coconut
1½ tablespoons melon seeds
1 tablespoon sesame seeds
10 cloves
6 green cardamom pods
½ cup cashew nuts
2½ tablespoons red chilli powder
1½ teaspoons poppy seeds
4 (2.5-cm) cinnamon sticks
1 tablespoon black cumin seeds
1 tablespoon black peppercorns

Method

- Marinate the fish slices in salt, turmeric and lime juice for an hour.
- For the spice paste, heat the oil in a frying pan or griddle; fry the spices till fragrant. Cool and grind to a fine paste.
- Heat 2 tablespoons oil in a frying pan; fry the fish slices on both sides. Remove and set aside.
- Heat the remaining oil in a wok; add the browned onion paste, spice paste and goda masala and sauté till the oil separates.
- Add very little water to make a thick gravy and cook for a couple of minutes. Add the fried fish and cook for 2 minutes.
- Serve with phulkas or rice.

Serves 6

NAGPURI DAHI MUTTON

MUTTON IN YOGHURT CURRY

This is probably the mildest Nagpuri dish I have encountered. The gravy is made up of not only yoghurt made from buffalo milk, but also some cream, cashew nuts, sesame and poppy seed pastes, that not only add richness to the dish but also tones down the fire of the chilli so liberally used.

Ingredients

1 tablespoon poppy seeds
1½ teaspoons sesame seeds
1½ teaspoons cumin seeds
1½ teaspoons coriander seeds
1½ tablespoons Garam Masala (page 34)
250g yoghurt, whisked
1½ tablespoons red chilli powder
1½ tablespoons ginger-garlic paste
Salt
Juice of 1 lime
1kg mutton on the bone, cut into 5-cm pieces
½ cup ghee
¾ cup Browned Onion Paste (page 103)
150ml cream

Method

- Dry-roast the poppy seeds, sesame seeds, cumin and coriander seeds in a frying pan or griddle till fragrant. Cool and grind to a fine powder. Mix the spice powder together with the garam masala.
- In a bowl, combine the yoghurt, ground spice mixture, chilli powder, ginger-garlic paste, salt and lime juice. Add the mutton, mix well and leave to marinate for at least 1 hour.
- Heat the ghee in a pan; add the onion paste and sauté for half a minute. Add the marinated mutton and 2 or 3 cups water and cook on low heat till the mutton is tender and the gravy thick.
- Stir in the cream and simmer for 2 minutes.
- Serve hot with rice, roti or bhakri.

Serves 6 to 8

VARHADI MUTTON

MUTTON CURRY WITH PEANUTS AND FENUGREEK LEAVES

Originating in the Vidarbha region of Maharashtra, this dish can be considered to be a cousin of Saoji Mutton. While many of the spices remain the same, dried fenugreek leaves, peanuts, millet (bajra) flour and gram flour add a different dimension and texture.

Ingredients

1½ tablespoons cumin seeds
1 tablespoon ginger-garlic paste
1 cup chopped fresh coriander
½ cup grated dried coconut
1½ tablespoons poppy seeds
2½ tablespoons raw peanuts
6 onions, 2 sliced and 4 finely chopped
1 tablespoon dried fenugreek leaves
3-4 tablespoons groundnut oil
1½ teaspoons roasted gram flour
1½ teaspoons roasted pearl millet flour
1 tablespoon Goda Masala (page 33)
1½ teaspoons coriander powder
1 tablespoon cumin powder
1½ tablespoons red chilli powder
1 tablespoon Garam Masala (page 34)
1½ teaspoons turmeric powder
1kg mutton on the bone, cut into 5-cm pieces
Salt
Fresh or dried red chillies, to garnish

Method

- Grind the cumin seeds, ginger-garlic paste and fresh coriander to a fine paste.
- In a pan, dry-roast the coconut, poppy seeds, peanuts and 2 sliced onions till the onions and coconut turn brown. Cool and grind to a fine paste with the dried fenugreek leaves.
- Heat the oil in a pan; add the 4 finely chopped onions and sauté till brown.
- Add both the spice pastes and the remaining ingredients, except the mutton and salt, and sauté till the oil separates.
- Add the mutton and salt and sauté till the mutton is coated with the spices. Stir in 2-3 cups water, cover the pan with a tight fitting lid, and cook on a low heat till the mutton is tender and gravy thick.
- Serve hot, garnished with red chillies.

Serves 6 to 8

VARHADI KOMBDI

SMOKED CHICKEN CURRY

When my younger son Shaan was about eight years old, he went through a 'chicken only' phase. No meal – including breakfast – seemed complete to him without chicken on the menu. Then, just as suddenly as this obsession had appeared, it disappeared. Now, Shaan cringes at the very thought of chicken, barring one dish. You guessed it! Varhadi Chicken. Though the spices make his eyes water, he relishes every bite of it till his plate is licked clean.

Ingredients

2 teaspoons turmeric powder, divided
1kg chicken, cut into 8-12 pieces
4 white Roasted Onions (page 42)
1 cup fresh coriander
2-3 tablespoons groundnut oil
4 bay leaves
1½ tablespoons ginger-garlic paste
1½ tablespoons red chilli powder
Salt
A piece of charcoal, for smoking
Thin strips of ginger, to garnish

SPICE PASTE

15 dried red Kashmiri chillies
½ dried coconut, grated
1½ tablespoons poppy seeds
1½ tablespoons star anise
1½ tablespoons cloves
1½ tablespoons black peppercorns
1½ tablespoons black cumin seeds
1½ teaspoons nigella seeds
½ nutmeg
½ teaspoon green cardamom pods

Method

- Rub 1 teaspoon turmeric powder all over the chicken and leave to marinate for at least 1 hour.
- Chop the roasted white onions and grind with the remaining turmeric powder and coriander leaves to a fine paste.
- For the spice paste, dry-roast all the ingredients in a frying pan or griddle till fragrant. Cool and grind to a fine paste.
- Heat the oil in a pan; add the bay leaves, ginger-garlic paste and both the ground spice pastes and sauté till the oil separates.
- Add the chilli powder and salt and stir to mix. Add the chicken and stir till well coated with the spices. Pour in 2 cups of water and cook on a low heat till the chicken is tender.
- Heat the coal on an open flame till red hot and place it in a small heatproof bowl. Place the bowl in the pan with the chicken and cover tightly with a lid for 5 minutes to flavour the chicken.
- Serve hot, garnished with ginger strips.

Serves 8

NAGPURI METHI KOMBDI

CHICKEN CURRY WITH FENUGREEK

This dish was made on special occasions in the Wada, our ancestral mansion in Pune. Chicken and fenugreek in a coconut curry with the unmistakable fragrance of dried lichen was a treat to remember.

Ingredients

1kg boneless chicken breast, sliced
1½ cups finely chopped fenugreek leaves
1 tablespoon ginger-garlic paste
2 teaspoons cloves
2 teaspoons black peppercorns
1½ tablespoons dried lichen
4 tablespoons groundnut oil
1 cup roasted dried coconut paste
1½ tablespoons coriander-cumin powder
Salt

Method

- Marinate the chicken in a mixture of the finely chopped fenugreek leaves and ginger-garlic paste for 4 hours in a refrigerator.
- Grind the cloves, peppercorns and dried lichen with a little water to a fine paste.
- Heat 2 tablespoons oil in a pan; add the marinated chicken and sauté for a few minutes. Add the spice paste and 1 cup water and cook, covered, till the chicken is tender.
- Heat the remaining oil in another pan; add the coconut paste, coriander cumin powder, salt and cooked chicken. Cook till the gravy is thick.
- Serve with rice, bhakri or roti.

Serves 6 to 8

NAGPURI KALA PULAO

BLACKENED MUTTON PULAO

This recipe is a speciality of the Bhosale family of Nagpur, a branch of the family of the great Maratha warrior king Chhatrapati Shivaji Maharaj. One of the most important ingredients of the dish is niger seeds, known as karale or khurasni in Marathi. Charred ingredients - coconut, poppy seeds and onion - contribute to the dark colour and very distinctive flavour of the dish.

Ingredients

½kg long-grained rice
10 cloves
5 black cardamom pods
10 green cardamom pods
5 (2.5-cm) cinnamon sticks
3-4 bay leaves
4 tablespoons ghee
5 onions, dry-roasted and ground to a paste
1 tablespoon ginger-garlic paste
1½ cups yoghurt, whisked
2 tablespoons Garam Masala (page 34)
Salt
1kg mutton, cut into 5-cm pieces
1 cup fried onions

SPICE PASTE

1 tablespoon ghee
½ cup grated dried coconut
1 tablespoon poppy seeds
1 tablespoon black sesame seeds
1½ tablespoons niger seeds
½ teaspoon nigella seeds
1 tablespoon red chilli powder
1 tablespoon coriander seeds
1 teaspoon black cumin seeds

Method

- Place the rice in a pan with water to cover; add the cloves, green and black cardamoms, cinnamon and bay leaves, and cook till the rice is half done. Drain.
- For the spice paste, heat the ghee in a frying pan or griddle; sauté the ingredients till fragrant. Cool and grind to a fine paste.
- Heat 3 tablespoons ghee in a heavy-bottomed pan; add the ground onion paste, ginger-garlic paste, ground spice paste, whisked yoghurt, garam masala powder and salt. Sauté till the ghee separates.
- Add the mutton and about 2 cups water. Cook on low heat till the mutton is tender and the gravy is thick and clings to the meat.
- Spread the fried onions on top of the meat. Layer the partially cooked rice on top of the onions.
- Heat the remaining 1 tablespoon ghee and sprinkle over the rice. Cover the pan and seal tightly with wheat flour dough or aluminium foil. Place it on a griddle and cook on low heat for 45 minutes.

Note: Roast the poppy seeds and dried coconut till they turn black to get the desired colour of the gravy.

Serves 4 to 6

NAGPURI KOMBDI MASALA

CHICKEN CURRY WITH MUSTARD AND CORIANDER

Garam masala is considered such an obvious ingredient in almost all Nagpuri dishes, that anyone sharing a recipe with you doesn't bother to mention it – just as people don't mention salt when orally sharing a savoury recipe. However, in this recipe, the garam masala is genuinely absent. A special spice blend is prepared which includes mustard seeds and fresh coriander. And though most people like to eat the curry with rice bhakri, I think nothing goes better with it than ragi bhakri (finger millet flatbreads).

Ingredients

4 tablespoons groundnut oil
3 large onions, sliced
½ dried coconut, grated
1 tablespoon split Bengal gram
1 tablespoon raw rice
1 tablespoon mustard seeds
1 tablespoon ginger-garlic paste
1½ teaspoons turmeric powder
1½ tablespoons red chilli powder
1 tablespoon coriander powder
1½ tablespoons cumin powder
Salt
1kg boneless chicken breast, sliced
1 cup finely chopped fresh coriander

Method

- Heat 1½ tablespoons oil in a frying pan or griddle; sauté the sliced onion, coconut, split Bengal gram and raw rice till onions and coconut turn brown. Cool and grind to a paste.
- Heat the remaining oil in an earthenware cooking pot or a heavy-bottomed pan. Add the mustard seeds, and when they start to crackle, add the ginger-garlic paste and sauté for a few seconds.
- Add the turmeric powder, chilli powder, coriander powder, cumin powder, salt and ground spice paste, and sauté till the oil separates.
- Add the chicken, chopped coriander and 2 cups water and cook, covered, till the chicken is tender and gravy thick.
- Serve hot with ragi bhakri, roti or rice.

Serves 6

SAOJI MACHHI FRY

SPICY BATTER-FRIED FISH

Rohu or carp is a freshwater fish which is ideal for this recipe. Encased in a spicy gram flour batter, this is a popular snack which goes well with drinks.

Ingredients

1 tablespoon gram flour
2 onions, ground to paste
1½ tablespoons Goda Masala (page 33)
1½ tablespoons red chilli powder
1.25-cm piece ginger
3 garlic cloves
½ teaspoon cumin seeds
½ teaspoon dried fenugreek leaves
1½ teaspoons coriander-cumin powder
1½ teaspoons turmeric powder
Salt
Juice of 2 limes
3 tablespoons oil, plus for deep-frying
2 eggs, beaten
1kg Indian carp fillets

Method

- In a bowl, mix together all the ingredients except the oil, eggs and fish.
- Heat 3 tablespoons oil and stir it into the mixture.
- Add the beaten egg and enough water to make a thick batter. Add the fish fillets, coat with the batter, and set aside for 1 hour.
- Heat plenty of oil in a wok and deep-fry the fish, a few pieces at a time, till crisp and golden. Drain on absorbent paper and serve with a fresh salad.

Serves 6

Glossary

English	Hindi	English	Hindi
allspice	*kababchini*	Indian carp	*rohu*
almonds	*badam*	jaggery	*gur*
asafoetida	*hing*	kidney beans, red	*rajma*
bay leaf	*tej patta*	lime	*nimboo*
Bengal gram, split	*chana dal*	liver	*kaleji*
black cumin seeds	*shah jeera*	lobster	*shevand (M)*
black lentils, split	*urad dal*	mace	*javitri*
black lentils, whole	*sabut urad*	mackerel	*bangda (M)*
cardamom, black	*moti elaichi*	mango powder, dried	*amchur*
cardamom, green	*chhoti elaichi*	mango, unripe green	*kairi*
carom seeds	*ajwain*	melon seeds	*magaz*
cashew nuts	*kaju*	mint	*pudina*
cassia buds	*nagkesar*	mugwort	*maipatri (M)*
catfish	*singara*	mustard	*rai*
charcoal	*koyla*	mutton/goat meat	*gosht*
chicken, country	*desi murgh*	mutton/goat meat, minced	*kheema*
chicken	*murgh*	nigella seeds	*kalonji*
chickpeas	*kabuli chana*	niger seeds	*ramtil*
chillies, dried red	*sookhi lal mirch*	nutmeg	*jaiphal*
cinnamon	*dalchini*	pearl millet	*bajra*
clams	*tisrya (M)*	peppercorns	*kali mirch*
clarified butter	*ghee*	pigeon peas, split	*tuvar/arhar dal*
cloves	*laung*	pomegranate kernels, fresh	*anar ke dane*
coconut	*nariyal*	pomegranate seeds	*anardana*
coconut milk	*nariyal ka doodh*	pomfret	*paplet (M)*
coconut water	*nariyal paani*	poppy seeds	*khus khus*
coconut, dried	*kopra*	potatoes	*aloo*
coriander leaves	*hara dhania*	prawns	*jheenga*
coriander seeds	*dhania*	quail	*bater*
crab	*khekda*	raisins	*kishmish*
cream	*malai*	rice flour pancakes	*ghavan (M)*
cumin seeds	*jeera*	rock salt	*sendha namak*
curry leaves	*kadi patta*	saffron	*kesar*
dried lichen/black stone flower	*dagad phool/kalpasi*	seer fish/kingfish	*surmai*
drumstick pods	*saijan ki phalli*	semolina	*rawa/sooji*
egg	*anda*	sesame seeds	*til*
evaporated milk solids	*khoya/mawa*	sesame seeds, black	*kala til*
fennel seeds	*saunf*	shark	*mori (M)*
fenugreek leaves	*methi*	silver bar-fish	*karli (M)*
fenugreek leaves, dried	*kasuri methi*	snakehead fish/murrel	*maral*
fenugreek seeds	*methi dana*	sorghum	*jowar*
finger millet	*ragi*	spinach	*palak*
flatbread	*phulka/roti/chapatti*	spring onion greens	*hare pyaaz ki pattiyan*
flatbread	*bhakri (M)*	star anise	*chakri phool/badiyan*
garcinia indica	*kokum*	sugar	*cheeni*
garlic	*lasun*	sultanas	*munnaka*
ginger	*adrak*	tamarind	*imli*
goat spleen	*tilli*	tomatoes	*tamatar*
gram flour	*besan*	turmeric	*haldi*
green gram, split	*moong dal*	vinegar	*sirka*
green mango	*kairi*	wholewheat flour	*atta*
green peas	*matar*	wholewheat grains	*gehun*
griddle	*tawa*	wok	*kadhai*
groundnut/peanut	*moongphali*	yoghurt	*dahi*
Indian salmon	*rawas*	zanthoxylum rhetsa	*tirphal/teppal (M)*

Note: M=Marathi

All measures used in the recipes are level unless otherwise specified.
1 teaspoon is equivalent to 5ml
1 tablespoon is equivalent to 15ml
1 cup is equivalent to 250ml.